Have Faith
Live It, Speak It, Believe It & Survive

By
Marilyn Blank

PublishAmerica
Baltimore

PublishAmerica has allowed this work to remain exactly as the author intended, verbatim, without editorial input.

Hardcover 978-1-4512-1142-9
Softcover 978-1-4512-1143-6
PUBLISHED BY PUBLISHAMERICA, LLLP
www.publishamerica.com
Baltimore

Printed in the United States of America

Dedication

First and foremost, this book is dedicated to my Lord and Savior Jesus Christ. It is because of his love and grace that this story is possible. Next, my book is dedicated to my "Angel Kim" that always has my back and fights my battles right beside of me. Next, the book is dedicated to all the churches, family, friends, hand holders, prayer warriors and the very talented doctors and nurses which also include my friend and personal nurse Penny that helped me along with my life's journey. Also this dedication is to John, Linda, Amy, and Susie without their support this book would have never been completed. Last but not least this book is dedicated to Neil and Cindy because without their gift of my computer and printer this book would have never been started. Love and prayers' to all of you.

CHAPTER ONE

Where do I start? I guess the best place is with a little background information. I wasn't raised in a home where love, patience or kindness was ever shown. Never feeling safe, secure, appreciated or even wanted is how I would describe my childhood. The years spent with my stepfather were tough; he was a strict military man. He used discipline to break the spirit of what he perceived was a rebellious child. I saw a very angry man that used and abused me in various ways. As I went from a child to a young lady, the relationship and abuse only got worse; kids just tell "stories" to get attention, right? I was told no one was going to believe me. It was true, my mother didn't believe me, how could she. She lived with the fear of being hit, seeing her kids being hit, items thrown across the room and other forms of abuse. I continued to try to get her to believe me, to get her to love me, to receive acceptance from her. For some reason, I never did. Maybe she was just over whelmed. She was trying to make a family out of this mess.

We were so very poor and I was the middle child. I had an older sister and a younger brother. All close in years, all with different last names. Our family life created a situation making everything a competition between us. We were never given a chance to have any type of a healthy relationship. Karen, the oldest, was "the good one". She was often our caregiver. She did very well in school and always did what she was told. When she was older, she got a job and used her money to buy things my brother and I needed but would not have had without her. Then there was Mike, he was youngest, and their only "real child." He was also the big "sports kid." They were so proud of him. I was the shy, middle kid, the "plain Jane." I could have gone through most of my whole childhood without being noticed, except for the attentions of my step-father. I never played sports or got involved in any activities. I was never very smart and never had any real desire to be. When I got my first real job, it was working at a donut shop in Frederick, Md. I worked every chance I got and the money came in quite handy. One day, for reasons that were never explained, my step-father loaded my brother into the car and the two of them drove off. We did not see them for a very long time. This created a situation where the money I made was needed for food and rent. Close to me graduating high school, I was informed that my brother and step-father would be returning. They would be coming back into our lives as quickly as they left. WHAT WERE MY GOALS IN LIFE? There was only ever one. To get away from the crazy life I was living and to have a REAL family. I wanted to be a mommy with a story book family.

I met Bobby in April 1977. I was seventeen years old. My step father and brother had returned home and were now living with my mother and myself again. Two months after their return I graduated from high school and had a plan to get pregnant. Bobby and I found out we could get married without consent if I was pregnant. So after I graduated Bobby and I were married. The service was very simple, maybe ten people attended. Bobby wore a plain suit and I wore the same dress I had worn to my high school dance which we did not attend because we were conceiving our first child. That was the same dress I later wore to my sister Karen's wedding. Seventeen days after I turned eighteen, our first son was born. In 1979, our second son was born. Bobby's Mom and Dad were awesome. They were everything I had always dreamed a Mom and Dad should be. Jim and Shelva were so very nice and kind to me. Shelva took me to all of my medical appointments and would always take me out for lunch afterwards. She had a baby shower for us even though no one from my side of the family would attend and I didn't know anyone from their side of the family yet. When our place got too hot because we did not have an air conditioner, Jim and Shelva made sure we got one. I truly felt so blessed and so much happier than I had ever been in my whole life. However, the relationship between Bobby and I proved too difficult to hold onto. What was supposed to be my fairy tale marriage ended in a divorce. I now found myself with little Jimmy and little Jason and the loss of the Mom and Dad I had always wanted. I am so lucky and have to say even as I am writing this, I still am lucky enough to have Jim and Shelva in my life, though our relationship is very different than when I was married to their son. I must say however, in my heart, I do believe that they loved me then and still do to this day.

CHAPTER TWO

The next few years were very hard. Trying to provide a life for two young children and myself were almost impossible. I felt like I had really hit rock bottom when I had to go to the store and use food stamps to feed my children. There had been many times I had experienced the pain of hungry and I did not want my kids to know what that felt like. I was determined, somehow, to find a way to change our situation. I heard about a program where I could learn to be a nurse's aide. I felt like a door was being opened. On my first day of class I sat with several other girls about my same age. There was a bet made between us girls that I couldn't get this young guy sitting across the room from us to ask me out. I guess I was the one that was chosen for this bet because I was the only one that had been married, divorced and had two kids. It was assumed I was; let's just say walking on the wild side. It must have been my lucky day because that guy did ask me out for lunch and went out to dinner that evening as well. That guy's name was Rex and we became inseparable right away. We were living together by the time we finished the class. Rex went on to get a job working in the operating room at Frederick Memorial Hospital and provided in home health care services. I worked in a different hospital and nursing home settings. I liked my jobs, but not with a true passion.

One day I was reading the newspaper and came across an interesting ad. It was for a part time van driver in a program that provided services to the mentally ill. It was a psycho-social rehab program. I had no experience what so ever and up until that very minute, had never given a thought to that line of work. It was the strangest feeling. I somehow felt I was supposed to get this job. I couldn't understand this at all. The thought of working with the mentally ill scared me. I couldn't even drive my car with a lot of true skill let alone a big van with a wheel chair lift.

Whatever it was, it kept working on me. I truly felt that I was supposed to be doing that job. I went to apply and was asked if I had any experience, of course I had to say no. I was asked if I had the class licenses needed to drive the van, again I had to say no. I really had to sell myself. I explained that I really wanted the job and somehow felt I was supposed to be doing it. I couldn't believe it, but they understood me. They told me they would help me practice with their van and then transport me to take the licensing tests. It was then explained that once I got my licenses, I would be paid $4.00 an hour for this part time job. I still wanted this job so bad but had no idea why. How in the world did I ever think I would be able to take care of my two children on a $4.00 an hour part time job? But it was like I was being told "it will be ok, trust me". I went to take the test and failed; I failed before I got into the van to drive. You see I was to do a spot check before getting into the van to drive. The instructor told me that I had not kicked my tires hard enough and he failed me. I had to go back and explain that I had failed my test. They agreed to let me try again. The test was only given on Thursday's so the next week I tried and failed once again. This time the instructor said I had not checked the lights on top of the van, lights that were not even there! He explained that even though this van did not have the lights other vans do and I would need to check them. I was given a third try the next Thursday and finally passed! Yeah me! Within a very short period of time, I truly loved this job. I was going to work with a passion in my heart, working full time plus was given a big raise. Later I was given a chance to work in another area of the program. I was still working with the mentally ill but even more closely. I began teaching ADL's, activities of daily living. Later I began working with clients that were hospitalized and helped them get out into the community. My supervisor and I started a mobile treatment service going where ever we were needed to provide services to our clients. It didn't matter if it was at a bus station, or on the streets. As it turned out, I really had a talent for this kind of work, and I loved it.

CHAPTER THREE

In 1986, after Rex and I had been together for seven years, my step father asked Rex one day, "Are you two ever going to get married?" Rex replied "Yes, I guess so." The next thing I knew, the date was set and the plans were being made. Don't get me wrong, I could not have been happier we were getting married. You see, Rex had also come from a home life that, let's just say was not ideal and for most of the years we had together, Rex said he was never getting married. Rex never got down on one knee, in fact he never even asked me to marry him. One day he just came to me and said "Your step father wants us to get married, your mother and him are moving to Las Vegas in October, how does August sound?"

August it was. I went to Goodwill and found a beautiful white wedding dress for $25.00. We had six bridesmaids and six ushers, a best man with little Jimmy the best man's helper, a flower girl and Jason was the ring bearer. It was a picture perfect wedding that we planned and paid for all by ourselves. Shortly thereafter, we decided we wanted to work on that picture perfect family together. Rex was good to me and was a very good father to Jimmy and Jason. We decided we wanted to add to our family.

Just months after we were married, we purchased what was supposed to be our starter home. Twenty three years later it has been our only home. One year after Rex and I were married and ten years after my boys were born we had a beautiful daughter named Brittney

Dawn Blank and two years later, our son Joshua Rex Blank was born. When we brought Josh home from the hospital, it was actually on Brittney's birthday, she thought Josh was her very own special Birthday present. What a beautiful family, four awesome children complete with a Mom and Dad. Life was so good. From the time I was a little girl I had always wanted a real family and to be a mommy, my dreams were all coming true.

Life always throws curve balls and one was coming our way. One day, while at work, I got a phone call from the middle school. My son Jason had been hurt and I should go to Washington County Hospital right away. They thought he would be ok. When I arrive at the hospital, I found Jason with a leg that looked like something right out of a movie. His leg looked like a shark had taken a big bite out of it. As soon as Rex arrived at the hospital, we had a meeting with the doctor explaining how serious Jason's injuries were. He was going to require major surgery to repair his severed Achilles tendon. It was going to require two levels of stitches, sixty on each level. He would have a full length cast from his hip to the tip of his toe. The doctor said to repair that much damage it would be like sewing two pieces of jello together. Our lives were about to change drastically. We had been living life one way and now because two boys were playing around, knocked over a bookcase hitting Jason in the leg, our world would be turned upside down. After his surgery, Jason had several different casts, a lot of doctor appointments and a lot of rehabilitation on his leg. He was unable to return to school for a very long time. When he was ready, he could not ride the school bus because the cast had his toe pointed downward. The doctor said when there was bad weather he needed to stay home for precautionary reasons. If he were to slip and fall, there would be a slim possibility that his leg could be corrected again. As time went on I made the decision to give up the job I truly loved, paid very well, and provided our health insurance. I was also going to miss the state holidays and paid vacations I had become very use to, but family came first. My family always came first. After months of not working and the financial toll it was having on our family, I once again felt the need to somehow take care of it.

I was standing in my three car garage one day saying "Lord, what are we going to do? I need to take care of Jason. I would love to be home with Brittney and Josh but we have so many bills that need to be paid." I started thinking of what I could do with what I had to solve this situation. Daycare! I could open my own daycare and I would call it "Bundles of Joy". That is exactly what I did.

CHAPTER FOUR

Rex did not like the fact he no longer had a garage or a place to park his boat, but I was very proud of myself. I was one of the first people around to name a family daycare. To have a family daycare that was neither in the home nor in a basement was almost unheard of when I opened my beautiful day care. Nowadays, things like that are expected, but not back then. I took a lot of pride in the fact that I helped to raise the bar for the expectations of child care providers in my area.

While working from home, it gave me the ability to put more time and energy into the business I helped Rex start while we were dating. At that time it was not uncommon to find us working side by side in all kinds of weather. There were times our clothes and hair would freeze while working outside. I even learned to run a fork lift. The business really took off and it was now Rex's only employment. He had given up his other jobs and decided he really wanted to own his own business. He named the business Blank's Cleaning & Restorations and declared himself as owner and operator. The early years of the business required Rex to do a lot of the work himself or with just one other person. As Jimmy and Jason got older they were able to help do a lot of the physical labor while Rex would drive around looking for work and keep on top of the jobs. We were very lucky to have me at home answering the phone, work on scheduling and trouble shooting. The business continued to do very well. It has operated for over 25 years. As a family during that time, we were blessed. We took family vacations to the beach, made several trips out west to see the Grand Cannon, Yellow Stone Park, Mount Rushmore, Grand Tetons, etc. We experienced things many people were only dreaming about, especially if they had four young children.

Deep within my heart I knew we were blessed, but by what, by whom? I had not grown up with the opportunity to have a relationship with the Lord. I knew with all the good that I had in my life now, I was still missing something. There was something that was not quite right. I started having a true desire to gain some kind of knowledge about the Bible. Somehow, I felt before I could truly be a good and effective mom, I had to find out what this was all about. For the sake of my children, I needed to do this, but had no idea how. My only exposure to church had been when my parents dropped me off at vacation bible school which was their idea of free child care.

There was also a time when my mother and grandma took us to the Christmas Eve service. We sat in the back row. I remember hearing two women talking about how this one lady was wearing the same hat she had worn the week before. Even with this being my only memories of church, I still had a real desire to get an education in this area. You see, there was something else that happened when I was a little younger that I did not understand. It happened when Jimmy and Jason were still little, way before my life with Rex. My grandma, everyone called her Mammer became very sick with cancer. She had a lung and one of her legs removed. For months she laid in bed in terrible pain. Everyone kept talking to her about fighting to get well, staying strong. She would throw up this terrible green looking stuff. Mammer did not want to be in the hospital, she wanted to be in her own home. My mother stayed with her most of the time. No one ever talked about how sick she really was or ever talked about her dying. I always really loved Mammer, especially with my crazy childhood she was the only part that seemed somewhat normal. I remember one day a preacher, from the church we had visited on Christmas Eve, came by to visit with her. I guess someone must have called him. He went to Mammers bedside and they talked privately. When he left, my Mammer she was somehow different. I am not sure why or how, but something was surely different.

My mother said Mammer decided she wanted to go home to her own house that night. Mom asked me to stay with her for the night which of course I agreed to.

During my time with Mammer, I mostly sat with her on the bed and cleaned her up when she got sick. I had a conversation with her which at first felt very awkward and I was really struggling with. I said, "Mammer, are you afraid?" She said, "Of what?" I said, "Are you afraid to die?" She said, "Not anymore." I went on to tell her how much I loved her, how much we all loved her. I wanted her to know how hard it was to watch her keep fighting this cancer when she was so sick. I told her I thought we were being selfish to ask that of her. I shared with her how I knew she was so tired and how hard she had fought this long, hard battle and when she was ready it was ok to stop fighting, and just let go. She did not have to fight any more. Within fifteen minutes of me saying this to my most beloved Mammer, I saw all the pain and suffering leave her face and nothing but calm and peace remained. There was no fear. Now that I am older and have children, I would like to believe I am also a little wiser, but the truth is when I think about death I have fear. Whatever took her fear away, even at the very minute she was facing deaths door, she was at peace. I wanted to find out what that peace was.

CHAPTER FIVE

I started trying to read the bible. I guess the best way to describe what I felt was just plain stupid. How was anybody supposed to understand this? I attended a lot of different churches, shopping around. I would drag Rex and the children along and I started asking questions and searching for answers. Even if it was too late for me, I wanted to make sure my children had the opportunity to know the Lord. It was a process, but I now know what it means to be saved, to be a Christian and to have a personal relationship with my Lord and Savior. It was not too late for me after all.

The day I was saved was such an amazing day. There was an outdoor revival at a church in Boonsboro called Victory Baptist. It was not a church we attended at the time. The revival had a reenactment of Jesus being hung on the cross. Speakers had been placed around in a big huge tent and you could hear this banging sound coming from them. It was the sound of the nails going into Jesus' palms; it was as if I could feel his pain. I then understood the sacrifice the bible talks about and how Jesus had shed his blood for my sins. I stood there with a feeling I had never experienced before, or since. Before long there was an alter call. My daughter Brittney took me by the hand and looked up at me and said, "Come on, you know what we have to do." We went forward that day and were forgiven our sins. We were saved. I have been a changed person from that minute on. Brittney and I were baptized the next week at a church in Frederick Maryland the same church we had been married in. This was also the church Rex attended with his family as a child. Shortly after that we started attending Victory Baptist Church. This is where Josh would be saved and baptized.

Josh was so funny when he decided he wanted to be baptized in his suit. He was so proud of himself, and announced to everyone what day he was going to be baptized. He also asked everyone to come to his house afterwards he just forgot to tell me this plan. Josh announced his big news to his school teachers, bus driver, class mates, and neighbors, basically everyone he liked. He was saved, being baptized, and they should come to his house to celebrate. I finally found out his big plan at church when he made the big announcement after the service. He had a pretty good turnout at our house that day. It was interesting that I had made a big pot of vegetable soup the evening before and a big bowl of turkey salad and somehow we were able to feed everyone that showed up. That had to be by the grace of God.

Jimmy, Jason, Cassy and Raymond have all been saved as well and all but Raymond have been baptized. Oh, you don't know about Raymond and Cassy yet but you will shortly. Anyway, one of the first major things I had to learn was the Lord meets you where you are and then you grow from there. It does not matter what your background, your age, nothing matters, except you become a new person. I use to let memories of my childhood really bring me down. I would feel so ripped off and would think how it really sucked. I thought that I could never truly get past all of the terrible things and memories I carried with me on a daily basis. As my relationship with the Lord grew, my attitude began to change. I learned how to first forgive those that had caused me such pain and move past those times. All that "stinkin' thinkin' " stopped and I began to realize I became a wonderful mom and child advocate *because* of my childhood. All of the hugs and kisses I didn't receive as a child and didn't get to pass out were in me just waiting for my own children to come along. All the pats on the back, the words of encouragement were just bottled up in me waiting to have someone to pass them on too. I realized I had witnessed firsthand all the wrong stuff and had such a strong desire to do it the right way. I discovered I had become a pretty strong person and figured out my attitude was going to mean everything. It could make me, or break me. As I continued to grow in my relationship with the Lord I also figured out it really did not matter whose DNA someone had when the mother gives birth, it only matters they are created by a heavenly father. His DNA is all that matters.

What I did next, a dear friend of mine said you should never do. I asked the Lord to use me, to really use me for something to glorify him. I wanted my life to truly matter. I do believe everyone has a purpose for their life. A God given purpose they sometimes never figure out what it is. This could be for many reasons such as: they never try to or they do not open their hearts and ears when the Lord tries to point them in the right direction. I had always believed my purpose had something to do with children but I felt there was more to it. I saw an ad in the paper about becoming a foster care parent through the Department of Social Services. I thought "Thank You Lord this must be a sign." I then received a call from my GYN after a checkup and follow up due to some problems I was experiencing. This was my first experience with cancer. After a complete hysterectomy, my life went on and I continued with my desire to become a foster care parent. Rex went with me to all of the required classes to become foster care providers. We completed the classes and shortly thereafter started opening our home to children in need. Often to sibling groups which would have been split up into different homes because groups of children are harder to place together. When Rex would leave for work, he would never know what to expect when he got home. Our house was pretty small. It only had four bedrooms with one full bath and a half bath. Of course by this time, Jimmy and Jason were grown with families of their own. Brittney and Josh were awesome about opening their home and hearts to the children.

I remember the very first little girl, she was two years old. The call from social services came a few hours before our family was leaving for a two week vacation. Social services gave us permission to take her along on our trip if it was ok with us. They had no other providers available. We agreed and picked her up to go with us on vacation. Of course like most foster care children she had no belonging. We had to pick up things for her on the way. The little girl loved "the lotion" which is what she called the ocean. She could not say the word ocean so it became "the lotion". She also started calling me mommy. Of course, Brittney and Josh were caught off guard by this. Brittney was fine, but not my Josh. Josh looked at this little girl and told her that I was HIS mommy, not her mommy. However, by the next day he grew to love that little girl and all the other little ones that came into our family after her. Looking back, it is funny that one of the happiest times of my life turned out to be when my home was filled with many children, most of them close in age with different last names. Oh, we had our struggles. Making sure all of the new children had shoes, did we have enough seats in our vehicle, and how was the little town of Boonsboro, Maryland going to handle the white family taking care of "those children of color". Our little town, at that time, only had one fast food place, one bank, a hardware store, and the schools. The first thing my Josh and Brittney did was to lift the children of color onto their backs and walk up and down the street. They felt they were going to help educate our little town. The thought was maybe God was using us in this way, as well as day care and foster care.

Having a day care and providing foster care, I felt strongly that everyone should learn first aid and CPR. At first we went to other places to get and renew our certifications. Later, I started hosting CPR and first aid training parties in my home. I convince others to have such parties as well. My children followed suit and learned first aid and CPR as soon as they were old enough. We had alarms and smoke detectors in almost every room of the house. All cars had first aid kits in them. We were so very careful. During this time, even though it was not something we had considered when becoming foster care parents, we became aware that God had another plan. I will say it like a sign I once saw, God created them and we adopted them. A sweet, little girl we named Cassy and her little brother Raymond joined our other four children. We also added Colby who was not from social services, but homeless and needed a family to love and someone to love him back. That totaled seven children, a mom and dad all living in our little house.

CHAPTER SIX

September 8, 2006 was the day our world changed forever. We had gotten up early that Friday morning. This weekend was a special weekend in our little town known as Boonsboro Days with crafts, yard sales, food and fun. When we woke up that morning, we woke up to such a good life. After several years of trying to adopt Raymond and Cassy, they were finally legally ours. In June, Josh had graduated high school a year early, and after the last year he had, that was almost a miracle in itself. First, Josh had to get his appendix removed. He had complications from that and had another surgery. Not long after that, he wrecked his four-wheeler and needed surgery to put pins and a rod in his wrist. He somehow made it through all of those challenges. He walked on stage for his graduation, although he had not wanted to, but I explained how important it was for us to see him in his cap and gown getting his diploma. Later he was glad that he had agreed to do this. He was now planning to work towards taking over Blanks Cleaning and Restorations. August had been awesome we had enjoyed our family vacation, our first with Colby. Of course, we had to purchase an SUV so we would have room for us all to travel together. We celebrated Josh turning seventeen and Brittney turning nineteen. Josh loved the SUV we had purchased so much, he purchased one for himself.

Now back to September 8th. We were getting ready to have a family yard sale. Colby and Cassy had left for school, I was suffering from a terrible migraine, and Raymond was watching television, while Rex,

Brittney, and Josh started having the yard sale at a friend's house. Josh said he was not feeling very well but thought if he ate something he would feel better. He went to the store to get me some coffee, thinking that would help my migraine and was going to pick up something up to eat. After going to the store he returned home with Rex. Brittney waited at our friend's house with the yard sale stuff. The plan was for Rex to pick up some other items he wanted of his to take over to the yard sale. Josh got his bike out of the shed laughing, saying he was "going to clean it up and sell it to get some gas money." Remember, he had just purchased his SUV. He turned his bike upside down and started cleaning it. A neighbor was walking down the street and had waved at Josh, and Josh waved back. Before Mr. Howard walked two houses away, Joshua had collapsed and was lying on the ground. Keep in mind, Rex had only left Josh for no more than five minutes. He returns and finds Josh flat out on the ground by his bike. He screams so loud that Mr. Howard hears him as do I. I came running with the telephone in my hand and I called 911. Rex was screaming that "Josh was not breathing." I told him to take the phone so I could do CPR. I never found his pulse. Josh's next breaths were taken in heaven.

I had to bury my seventeen year old son, my own child I had given birth to. I wanted my whole life to be a mom and had worked very hard to be a good mom, I tried to be careful but somehow I had failed. When he needed me most, I had failed him. When he collapsed I started CPR right away, the way I had been trained all of those years, but I must have done something wrong. I tried so hard to stay calm and do what I needed to, maybe I should have yelled at Josh, so loud that he could have heard me and he would not have slipped away. He would still be alive I thought. If it had not been Boonsboro Days, help could have gotten there faster, maybe that would have made a difference. Yes, something like this can really make nasty thoughts come into a person's head. How dare God take my birth son away from me when I had just adopted two other children and taken in another? Three children that belonged to someone else and living in my house while I was forced to pick out a casket for my own son to be buried in the ground. How fair was that! To make matters even worse, when I needed

Rex more than any other time, depression consumed him to the point he was unable to function at all.

It did not take me to long to realize these thoughts would destroy anyone that allowed themselves to think that way for long. From the day one is born their days on this Earth are numbered. Josh did not leave this world one day sooner than he was supposed to. Lean not on your own understanding, which is what the Bible tells us. I was not going to be able to make sense and understand all of this. I was going to be stronger in my faith than ever, even when it would be tested over and over again. What I did know, and understand is that my beautiful son Joshua was a gift from God just like every child, he was on loan from God. Whatever Josh's purpose was in this world, it had been fulfilled and it was his time to leave Earth to go home to heaven. No, I did not find total comfort with all of this on that day. I still cry almost every day because I miss him so much. I know one day we will be together again when the Lord calls me home, whenever that may be. In the mean time, I decided I was going to live a life that my son would be proud of and would honor his memory. The days following Josh's death were so extremely hard. I kept thinking I had to get the jobs done and make Josh proud. I had to keep remembering Josh was a saved person so he was in a wonderful place called heaven. So as hard as it was to attend the viewing and funeral of my baby, I knew I was not saying goodbye forever, he was already in heaven waiting for me. It was just a shell that was lying in that casket.

CHAPTER SEVEN

Depression really controlled Rex at this point. He was unable to help make any of the funeral arrangements, help to make any plans, care or support the other children or even care for himself. He cried nonstop unless he took enough medication, which knocked him out and he slept. This was the beginning of my life, separate from my husband's. If Rex was asked to do anything he would say "I can't". For his every "I can't", it gave me something else to do. The thought of just getting the jobs done kept going through my head. It was so very hard. There was a long list of things needing to be done. It started the minute we left the hospital, after being told Josh had died. The first thing, I had to accomplish was going to the school to make sure his girlfriend heard the news from me. Other friends, family members had to be contacted as well. I had to plan the funeral, pick the casket, vault, music, clothes, and all other details. Rex stayed at home and was unable to cope let alone help.

Then there was the big question, what did Josh die from? We did not know. Of course, when something like this happens, all types of stories go around, most not very pleasant. The medical examinator asked a lot of questions and explained there would be an autopsy; it turned out to be more than one autopsy. First we were told they were unable to find a cause of death. After some time passed they reported they had tested Josh for all kinds of drugs and nothing was found, not even an aspirin in his system. The area was searched were he collapsed. The only thing that was found was the tire cleaner he was using to clean his bike. They determined Josh must have breathed in too much of the tire cleaner while hurrying to clean his bike and that was the cause of death. I contacted the tire cleaning company and asked for the spec sheet, I was determined no one else would die because of this product. The medical examiner office thought that the tire cleaner was not the cause of death. By this time, all of this was adding to our nightmare. How can we be told our son died from one thing and then be told no, it was not the cause of death after all. We had a discussion with our local funeral home and they had never heard of anything like this before. Notice I am saying we this and we that, it was not we, it was me. I was also dealing with phone calls at 2:00 a.m. asking if I would consider having Josh become an organ donor. It seemed as if that whole process took hours, but my answer had to be yes. Josh was always the kind of person that would help others whenever he could. He was kind, and a friend to all. He would never of said no if given the chance to say yes and change a life. Months later we received a letter saying two people who had been blind can now see, thanks to Josh. Another wonderful gift my son left behind.

There were constant details to attend to, company stopping by, phone ringing, and the laundry of course. We were dealing with seeing Josh's SUV sitting in the driveway and Colby not wanting to go into his bedroom because this room was the one he and Josh shared. Cassy needed to go back to school, Blank's Cleaning and Restorations still needed to operate. I continued to be in contact with the medical examiner's office to see if they had figured out the cause of death. I was being told no, it was not something with his brain, and instead it was something that happened real quick, right where he was, within seconds. On the morning Josh passed away, he said he was not feeling well and had bought one of those energy drinks while at the store. Rex kept the drink container for some reason. We wanted to know if they would test the drink, or if it was possible it could have had something to do with his death. Without hesitation they told us no. Recently there had been an article in the paper showing some evidence about deaths in younger people due to these types of drinks. I asked if they could send someone to our house thinking maybe it would be helpful to see the area and they refused. Rex thought it might be related to his truck running in the driveway since they were only going to be there a few minutes. We were all searching for answers.

On a particularly hard day, something happened which I never have forgotten. Rex came to me and asked for a hug. He said "he needed a hug." I asked him if he needed to hug me because he wanted to do that for me or if it was just all about him. I let him know if it was all about him and his needs only, I couldn't. I had no energy left and what little bit of life I had left, I wasn't going to let him drain it out of me on his selfish needs. We did not hug then and we still have not to this day. Rex remembers that as a day that I was not there for him. I was just so used up at that point I had nothing left to give. I was feeling so alone myself. The only time I was able to have any thoughts that really made any sense, were in the shower. Actually it was the only time I was alone with my thoughts. It was one of those alone times when I realized, as crazy and out of control life was, what a blessing Raymond and Cassy were. They were not just someone else's children, they were God's children. He trusted me enough to care and love them even at the most terrible time of my life. Or maybe he knew I needed them to love me like only children can during this time and for other issues I was about to face. I was trying hard to remember to thank the Lord everyday even in the most troubled times.

During one of my alone times in the shower, I remembered Josh telling me about a conversation he had with a teacher at school about telling people in your life how much you appreciate them. After that conversation, Josh decided he was always going to tell people how much he appreciated them. So, from that day until his last, Josh would always say "I appreciate you". I got so use to hearing that several times a day it taught me how to say it as well. I now make sure I say it to others; I hope I do not forget this lesson. While sitting here, I am crying, hearing those words in my mind. I am so proud of what kind of person my son had become. His teachers, doctors and parents of his friends were always telling me about how kind and respectable he was even before he passed away. To know him was to love him, and admire him. I am so grateful that I did not have to worry about his salvation. I knew he was in heaven.

Every day the thought still remained, why he was in heaven and not sitting across the dinner table from me. An idea came to me; maybe his computer or cell phone could shed some light on his death. I did not have any computer skills or knowledge of a cell phone at that time. So I found a local expert in the field to come to our house. I explained I needed to find out any information I could about my son. He had died very unexpectedly and we were trying to find out why. I gave him Josh's computer and cell phone but nothing he found shed any light.

Finally the day arrived when we received his death certificate in the mail. It said amended, date, time, place, cause. The cause was a big long name and I had no idea what it was. I called for an explanation and they told me it was a chemical. They informed me this chemical was found in computer cleaners. They believed Josh purposely breathed this computer cleaner. This was totally crazy. I tried to ask them questions like: how could they say they had to change the date, time, place, and cause of death? This was the second time the cause of death had been change. I knew when my son had died and where, how could they possibly change that? Also, they had previous said there was absolutely no drug of any kind in his system. There was no computer cleaner where Josh collapsed. Was Josh going to be smelling computer cleaner in his yard, while he was hurrying up to clean his bike for the yard sale? He was also just waving to his neighbor. None of this made any sense, but the medical examinator's office had reached their decision and did not want to discuss it any further. This was most certainly one of those times I was talking about, when your faith gets tested. Everyone was asking us "Did you find out what Josh died from yet?" We knew the medical examiner's office was wrong. Rex was really letting this consume him. He was not able to think about anything else. We started talking to a lawyer and I had gotten all the information about the time line for that day and the transcripts of the 911 call. A lot of my time was being put into this. I could not just fixate on this one thing though. I had to continue to take care of life and life's situations. It was fortunate I was able to do this.

I was sure that Josh was looking down on me and he was proud of how I was taking care of matters. My shower time was still my refuge.

I really looked forward to this time; it was a time and place to get away from the happenings of that minute. I always had to be prepared for where my thoughts might take me. At this point in time it was just to sort through my thoughts of Josh. I remembered a day Josh and I were talking. He had a one dollar bill in his hand and he ripped it in half keeping half and giving me the other. He said that way when we were not together, we could think of each other and know that the other person had the other half of what it took to make a whole. You see together we made a whole. I now felt really sad wishing I had remembered his other half of that dollar and buried it with him. One day I started thinking about when he got his driver's license, how happy and proud he was. Oh yes, Josh and his old mustang. He wanted to fix that car up and race it at the track. He was so proud when he purchased his SUV, what a smart move. The day he got the SUV, he came home to pick up Raymond and another buddy. He took them for a ride and then to do Raymond's next best thing went to Pete's Barber Shop for a haircut. The day before Josh passed away, he had taken his SUV to jiffy lube to have them check it over with one of those machines to making sure nothing was wrong with it that needed immediate attention. He was a very mature, responsible young man.

That is when my heart led me to make a decision. I read my bible and in there are many stories which are very hard to understand, but a true believer does. For instance when Mary gets pregnant and tells Joseph "although she had never had sex, she was going to give birth to baby Jesus, the savior of the world." At times, I was having an easier time understanding that story than why my seventeen year old son left Earth and went to heaven in a blink of an eye. My faith was going to bring me through these very hard times. I was not going to understand it all; I was never going to have all the answers but what I was going to do was be a Mary. I was not going to hide my face because of what bad things others might think about me or my son when I know the truth. I was going to live my life with purpose, always giving God the glory. I did not talk to the lawyer anymore; I did not waste any more of my time or energy on the cause of Josh's death. I was more concerned that others would someday be able to call heaven their permanent home. During this time, I met a wonderful lady named Arlene who showed me amazing strength. She had lost not just one son but two. One was due to a motorcycle accident and the other to a long illness but both were young boys. A strange twist, her angels were buried next to my Josh, three young boys beside each other, so much life cut short. Arlene came to my house after hearing about Josh's death even though we had never met. She started reaching out to others after feeling the pain of losing her own boys. When Arlene first came to my house we cried and cried together. She knew how I felt when no one else could, one mother to another. We have shared many tears together since that day, but it was through her love and compassion that I really started to heal. Arlene taught me; to start healing I had to reach out to others. There are so many other hurting people in this world and just maybe sometimes we can help each other. I did however get a little side tracked from this mission by something called cancer.

CHAPTER EIGHT

I had been suffering with migraines for quite some time and they had become very intense. My face had been hurting plus terrible nose bleeds. I would be fine one minute and the next minute I would be in terrible pain with blood just pouring out of my nose. I knew something wasn't right. I had just lost my baby Josh, my husband was so depressed, I was not sleeping and no matter how hard I tried, I could not get the world to stop long enough for me to catch up. Of course I didn't feel good and I was so very tired all the time.

There could not have been a worse time, but then there wouldn't have ever been a good time, for my Brittney to start having difficulties. I won't go into a lot of information about this, that will be her book to write, but she was having some serious health issues. So serious in fact, that one day I was on the way to one of my doctor's appointments and I got a call from Brittney's doctor regarding some of her test results. The doctor said he needed to see me right away. I turned around, cancelled my appointment and had a meeting with Brittney's doctor that same day. Brittney and I had to go back to the same hospital where her brother had just been pronounced dead only a few months earlier. Brittney had to have many same day surgeries before her situation was finally under control. Each of her surgeries was very scary to me, she would have to be under anesthesia and there was such fear each and every time she would go into the operating room holding onto one of Josh's shirts. Thank God Brittney's situation was improving but I kept getting worse.

I could not work any longer; I had to close my day care. I was going from one doctor to another. I started with my family doctor, who sent me to an ENT from the ENT to a blood doctor then to the Good Samaritan Hospital. One place to another, one doctor after another, I was truly getting worn out. One day I was sent to a place I had been over a dozen times before, but when I entered that day, I became so confused I did not know where I was. I had no idea how to even get to my doctor's office. Security had to help me find my doctor's office. I was told it was because I was not sleeping and due to the extreme stress I was under. By Christmas, I was so weak and tired; I could not hold my arms above my head for more than a few minutes at a time. It was pure determination but after a full day, the Christmas tree was finally up. This was followed by a lot of crying when I had to then figure out which would cause less crying, hanging Josh's Christmas stocking or not.

The Christmas after Josh passed away I just knew was going to be awful but I was so wrong. The community rallied around us to make sure the children still had Christmas and we as a family still had food and comforts. But once again it went way beyond that. I have to give examples of the most wonderful Christmas of my lifetime. The week before Christmas Nora Roberts invited our family plus a few other families from our community to a Christmas party right here in our town. Nora Roberts writes books and some have been turned into Lifetime movies, but she does a lot for her own community. I wasn't aware she did things like that until she included our family in this event. She never advertised that she was helping folks in this manner but how else can people that are not working and that are down and out or that are going through a very difficult time attend a Christmas party? Santa was there, pictures were taken and there was a lot of good food. There were even some very special gifts.

We received a phone call asking if Santa could come to our house for a visit. I said "Of course!" I wanted the kids to feel as much joy as possible, where ever possible during the most difficult time of our lives. I got another call asking if this visit could happen on Christmas Eve. Like I said, I was expecting this to be the hardest time of my life but the only way to describe it is magical. When it was time for Santa to arrive for his visit my children started looking out the window. I noticed a car had pulled up in front of our house, and then another car, and then another car. Raymond and Cassy spotted Santa and Mrs. Claus, the elves and more and more people. They all started walking into the house carrying gifts. Some of the people headed toward the kitchen our table was filled with boxes of food. Everyone gathered in the living room around the Christmas tree. There were people everywhere, sitting on the floor, steps etc. Cassy and Raymond were just bouncing with joy. We were given gifts to open. Raymond would ask for everyone to close their eyes until he opened his, he wanted to make sure the gift was not something like underwear first. Then everyone would open their eyes and Raymond would ask Santa if there happened to be another present for him. When the gifts were all opened, we all sang Christmas songs. Christmas spirit and Christian love just filled our home. Thanks to Pleasant Valley Baptist Church, this was the most beautiful memory for my family and me.

Times like these really change people, well most people, some more than others. It was around the Christmas season that I was finally told I had a very rare condition called relapsing polycontritist. Wow, what a name. At least my condition has a name so maybe just maybe something could be done about it to make me feel better soon. Doctors are finally saying it is not just stress and I know now that it is not all in my head. I should have known that anyway, I am a lot tougher than that. During the time I was seeing the ENT's and other doctors there had been tests for cancer run, and I was told I did not have cancer. Finally after many months of going to all those other doctors and hospitals, I am sent to John's Hopkins in Baltimore Maryland. Many more tests were run, including a few new cancer tests. Now, after all of these months, I found out that I did have cancer. I have had cancer the whole time, and now it is almost too late. Just six months after I lost my precious son, I am told I have a very rare form of cancer. It is so rare, in fact, including my case it has only been reported two times. (That has changed now, that I have been added the medical journal) My cancer is called basal bid squamious cell caranama masquerading as rosacea. Death, death is already so new and real and fresh to my family. In fact, the headstone was just being placed on Josh's grave. Poor Brittney, she had just lost her baby brother who was also her best friend, fighting her own health demons and now my cancer. Then there was Colby, who had been failing all his classes in school before coming to live with us. Now had worked his way back where he was hopefully going to graduate in a few short months, I had to make sure that was still going to happen. Poor Raymond and Cassy, were only five and six at the time and had already experienced every bad thing life could have dished out. As for Rex, he was still basically checked out of everything. Thank God for Kim, more on her later. Ok, now what? I could not believe this was a part of God's plan for me but if it was, I was preparing myself for it. I knew God was always in control. I was going to continue to do what I had set out to do when Josh passed away. I was going to make him proud and glorify God. I was actually given the news that I had cancer over the phone from my family doctor. It was not easy news for my doctor to tell me and it was not easy for me to hear. As she told me she started to cry right along with me. I made her repeat what she was saying to me several times and I had asked her to hold on as I got a piece of paper so I could write down what she was saying. When I got off the phone the only thing I had written on the piece of paper was "believed to be staged four cancer" Rex was standing beside me when I got off the phone and asked what the doctor said. I told him to wait a minute and I went into the bathroom. I cried for about two minutes, said the word cancer and walked back out. I guess Rex had read the paper by that point. He was saying things like "why", "this sucks", "this isn't fair", I said, "It will be ok". I wanted nothing more in this world than to have those words said to ME.

It was now the end of March 2007. Things were happening really fast now; this was not a new thing for me. Johns Hopkins called and I was given a list of appointment to go to. At this point I didn't know what was facing me, or what it even meant to have this kind of cancer. What kind of treatments would I need? When I was given a list of the appointments I didn't really understand nor did I question too much at that point what each one of these appointments were. I figured I would ask any and all questions when I got to the appointments.

Two very close, dear friends offered to go with me to these appointments which had all been scheduled for the same day. My friends had no idea what they had gotten themselves into. It turns out the appointments were out of order and the first appointment was with someone that wanted to make a mold of my nose so that if and when the time came, a plastic surgeon could build me a new nose to look like my old one. It could also be used to make some kind of fake nose. "What! What!" I can't understand, what is being said? This man is saying something wrong. No one had said anything about taking my nose off! This man is saying something about options; when the time is right, I can have a nose again. I already have a nose! My friends tried to calm me down. They seemed to understand the words that came from this man's mouth, and only one of my friends is a nurse. Calm down nothing, I am handed a book and am told I can look at this book and see what the future can hold for me. One day I can have a nose again, look at this book, NO THANKS!!! I sat there and knew in my heart that regardless of what words were coming out of my mouth I would do whatever they asked. I did not have the presence of mind at that point to do anything else and the mold of my nose was made. I then walked to my next appointment. This is the appointment that should have been the first appointment. It was then explained that if I wanted to live, I must have surgery and it would require my nose being totally removed and the left side of my face would also be affected. I would be left with a big hole in my face. It is unknown whether they will even be able to get all of the cancer out or what else may be affected. I have no options, except death.

My new doctor was Dr. Patrick Byrne. We found each other almost by chance, after all the misdiagnoses of the other doctors, here he was. I am so thankful that I found myself sitting there in his office with my friends. I actually had started out with another doctor at Johns Hopkins which started testing and had brought Dr. Byrne in on my case. Together, the two of them decided to rerun the test for cancer. Sure enough in no time the results were back and the race was on to save my life. I truly felt that it was God that hand delivered me right to this doctor. When my life was so very crazy and out of control, Dr. Byrne always seemed to be just the opposite. He was always calm, quiet spoken and always, ALWAYS in control. We made a pact right from the start to be upfront and straight forward with each other. Dr. B., as well as my whole team, always made time for me. They always answered all of my questions and many times it was the same questions over and over again.

CHAPTER NINE

April 3, 2007 was another one of those life changing days. My family was there, Rex, Brittney, Jason, his wife Nicole, my friend Kathy and Amber (she had been Josh's girlfriend). There were seven people in room seven. I also knew people all over the world were praying for me. Up until this day, I had never been able to pray out loud, not when anyone else could possibly hear me. However, something happened that day, I do not know when I got the confidence or even the words to speak that day but things just seemed to flow. While everyone was gathered in my room before surgery I asked if we could all have prayer together. No one resisted, even though there were doctors, anesthesiologist, nurses; everyone joined in. I explained that I knew I was going to be alright, one way or the other, that I was a true believer in the Lord Jesus. I also said that I believed each member of my team in that room had a special talent that God had given them. They were going to use their talents that day to perform surgery and I wanted us all to thank God in advance for what was about to happen. AMEN. Calm then came over me and that was all I remember about my first surgery.

The next morning can only be described as unbelievable. Of course, I was bruised and swollen and could not see out of my eyes, which turned out to be a blessing. I was given a tray of food to eat which was a hamburger and smiley fries on it. What a joke that was. I could not open my mouth wide enough to take a bite of anything and someone thought I could eat a hamburger. I felt lucky the day when a straw fit between my teeth enough so I could take a few swallows of some juice. The nurse came in and told me my surgery had been about twelve hours or so. I knew that it was sometime after 7:00 pm before I had gotten back to my room. The nurse said I needed to get up and walk to the bathroom. She helped me get up and I made my way into the bathroom and found myself in front of a mirror. I then got my first look at the new me. What a shock when I looked at my face I looked terrible! Imagine a woman looking like that but I then had another shock I was being released from the hospital. Only hours after my nose was removed I was being discharged from the hospital, unbelievable. What happens if something goes wrong? If I got home and had to call 911 would they even know what to do. I have no nose and half my face is gone, how would anyone know how to do CPR? None of this seemed to matter; I was on my way home.

Marilyn, plain Jane Marilyn, the girl that never stood out in a crowd and always blended in was changing fast, and for all the wrong reasons. I had never seen anyone without a nose before and now, one was looking back at me every time I looked in the mirror. And then there was the issue of my face, it looked pretty messed up. The day after I got home I called my dad, I mean my birth father not my step father. My step father and my mother had both passed away within the last few years. Anyway, I called my dad and I told him," This is the ugliest thing I have ever seen". He said something to me that changed me forever, inside and out. He said, "Don't you ever say that again, You go to the window, look outside and say thank you Lord thank you for giving me the chance to wake up and see my children again; to hug them, to kiss them. Thank you for the sun and the birds, thank you Lord." He then said, "This is what a cancer survivor looks like today." My dad was so right. I had to get the right attitude. I was going to be a survivor. I was not going to be a victim and I was going to remember to thank the Lord each and every day I was given from then on.

Not long after I got home I knew I was going to be dealing with this cancer for quite some time, that is if I was blessed enough to have a future. I decided to make my funeral arrangements just in case. If the Lord should call me home I needed things to be taken care of. I did not want my family needing to make any arrangements for me since they had been through so much already. I started planning the second funeral in six months, this time it was my own. I decided where my service should be, who would preach the sermon, what music was to be played, and purchased new clothes with a pin attached saying BELIEVE and of course I would be laid to rest beside my son Josh. My name was added to the headstone including my birth date. The only thing missing was the date of my death. My plan was for that was to be as far off in the future as I could make it for the sake of my children. I was going to make sure things were as easy as possible for those I was leaving behind. I made sure in every way I could that my children would be just fine. Rex told me he would not be able to care for Raymond and Cassy and I agreed with him. He told me that I needed to find someone that would take care of them should something happen to me. I did find someone, or let's say we found each other. Rex called a lawyer and he came to the house with all the paper work before I left to go to Johns Hopkins for one of my surgeries. After the lawyer arrived I was told we needed two witnesses. I called two of our neighbors and they came over to be our witness's and the papers were finalized.

It was so hard for my little Raymond and Cassy. It would break my heart to think about what they were going through. Their lives had already been so bad, they had been abused, and neglected and only God knows their whole story. They ended up in foster care at the age of one and two. We finally were able to adopt them and within a few short months, their new brother passed away. It was one major problem after another. Rex and his depression, Josh passing, Brittney and her illness and now I am sick. They were known as special needs children when we adopted them. I could only see angels, however now it was becoming very obvious that Raymond was going to have a lot of issues that needed to be addressed. Poor Raymond, as if things were not bad enough. The time approached when he was to start kindergarten. Kindergarten was not ready for Raymond any more than Raymond was ready for Kindergarten. His teacher tried but it was a very long year for us all. Even with the school being aware of everything Raymond was dealing with in his young life, I was hearing about how Raymond just had to learn to behave. Raymond had experienced every bad thing the world could dish out, he had just witnessed his brother dying right in front of him, and he was scared the same thing was going to happen to his mom. It was also documented that Raymond had ADHD and determined later that Raymond has sensory sensitivity issues. Anyway, to make this long story short, Raymond was in the principal's office on the first day of school and many days thereafter. He was later suspended from kindergarten and I was asked to send him to another school, one that was for children with behavioral problems and I refused to do that. It was a very crazy time. I was fighting like crazy to find a way to help my child. It was in many ways exactly what I needed to be doing at that time. There is no better way to keep a fire stirred up in a mother than having to fight for her baby.

Cassy seemed to be doing ok. Her grades were good. However I remember one day when she came home from school and she just broke down and cried. I asked her why she was crying. She said she had lost part of her recess because I had forgotten to sign her test. Her grade on the test I had forgotten to sign happened to be an A by the way. I called the school and was told all the children had to remember to have their papers signed, it showed they were responsible. I explained to the teacher and to the school councilor how bad this made me feel, that it was my fault and I was told it was Cassy's responsibility to remind me. People had no idea what my life was like. The councilor did say something that was very helpful. I told her how bad I felt because ever since I had adopted the children, my life was turned upside down and crazy. She said that the children were very young and hopefully this time of their life would only be such a small amount of time out of what will hopefully be a long life. I felt my major job was suppose to be that of some kind of super mom and now just the little simple things like remembering to sign a test were being forgotten. It was usually these little simple things that would occur that would break me. Most of the time I would appear to have everything under control. I had to make the rest of the family think I was fine, they were fine and that life was going to be great. It was pretty hard sometimes to pull this off when I had to face life with most of my face gone. There would be times when I would break down, this didn't happen often but when I would, it would be a major break; it would never be in front of my family only my closest friends.

How was I going to be remembered? I really didn't have anything to leave behind, nothing anyone would be thrilled to receive. I didn't have money, or fancy belongings and it was possible without either Rex or I working we could even lose our house. So what did I have to leave behind for my love ones to remember me by? I have always had a passion for kids. During the years I worked in this field I tried to have rules and laws changed regarding foster care and adoption, however I doubt I will be remembered for that. I used to measure my success by how my kids were doing. When Jimmy and Jason finished school, got married, and had my beautiful grandchildren I felt somehow that was my success. Brittney and Josh both graduated at sixteen and I could not have been more proud. Colby was on his way to graduation but now as I faced the reality of death I realized that those things were their successes, but what was my life going to stand for when I am no longer in this world, how will I be remembered?

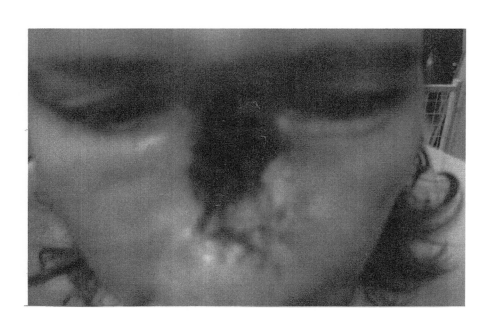

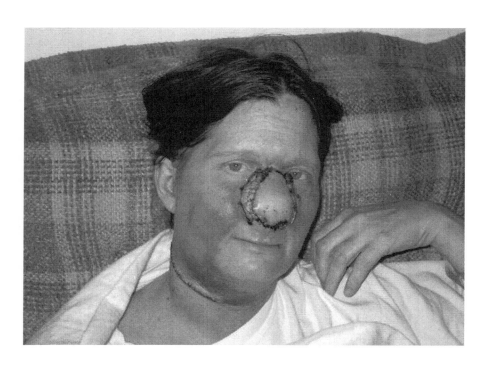

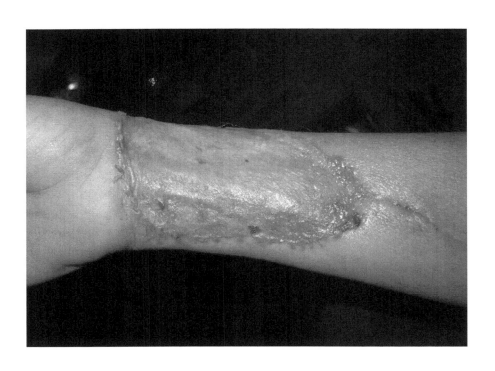

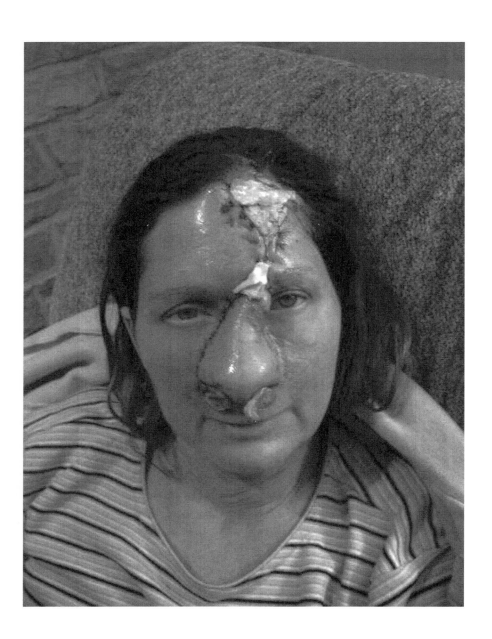

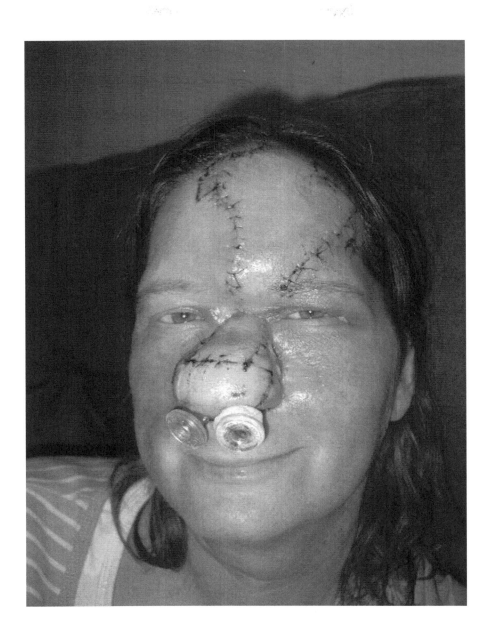

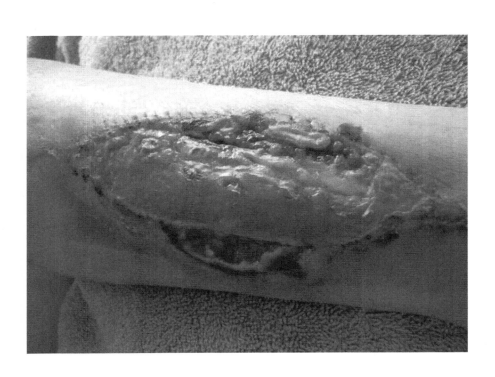

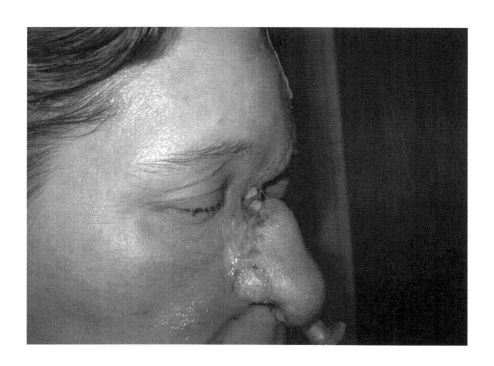

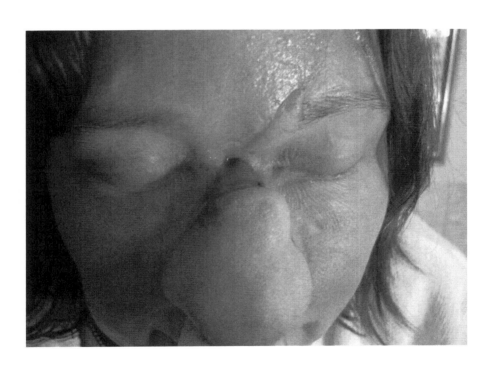

CHAPTER TEN

A Life to Be Remembered

I wanted to live my life TO BE REMEMBERED. I wanted to be remembered as someone who loved her children, grandchildren and all children with a passion.

I wanted to be remembered as someone that was good and kind and tried to always help others. I wanted to give people the courage to face their hard times and find joy while doing that. I wanted to always set a good example for what a good person should be, and be one that my kids, grandkids and loved ones could be proud of. I wanted to strive to do the right thing even when the right thing was the hard thing to do.

I did not want to waste my life. God only gives each person one life, it is up to each person to decide how they will spend their days

This is what I hope to leave behind.

I was now going to really put all of this to the test facing the next major step. Since my April surgery the plan was to heal enough so it could be decided what the next necessary treatment would be. They had told me my only option would be radiation treatments. There was nothing else to try. Chemotherapy would not work on my type of cancer. Of course I didn't want to have Chemo anyway but it was a terrible thought that the only option to safe my life was radiation. I had always been told, "Don't put all of your eggs into one basket"; somehow this is exactly what I felt I was doing. This new life's journey was one I would not have to travel alone. God put an amazing angel into my life to travel this path with me. Her name is Kim, who was Rex's cousin. She came to my house one day and we started talking and I was able right off the bat to show her a side of me others very seldom saw. I said, "How in the world am I ever going to be able to go through this?" Without skipping a beat Kim looks at me and says, "We will do it together." Up until that day Kim and I had never spent much time together, hardly knew each other at all, but that was all about to change and very quickly.

We started off by checking into what kind of radiation treatments I should receive and where the best place for me to receive the treatments. After many hours of research, and a lot of phone calls we decided my aggressive, rare kind of cancer should be battled in a very aggressive manner. We interviewed the staff and decided this battle would be best fought at John Hopkins even though this meant a lot more traveling time. The plan was made from day one that I was not going to be doing the driving; my angel was going to be behind the wheel. We found out I was going to be scheduled for thirty three treatments. Then we were given the news that before the radiation could begin I needed to see a dental specialist. There was a lot of dental preparation that was necessary due to the angles and areas that the radiation needed to cover. My back teeth on both sides, upper and lower had to be removed as well as any weak or cracked teeth. Kim took me to all of those appointments even though she had put off her own dental care due to her fear of dentists.

The next day after the dental work was completed and the day before the radiation treatments, there was yet another step to be taken. The MASK had to be made; there is nothing good I can say about that whole experience. The mask was a cover that was made to fit over my face so it could be marked where I was to receive the radiation. I would have to wear it every day during my treatment. My face already hurt so badly. Add the fact that the dental work had just been done made the situation worse. The hole in my face had to be packed; stuffed with gauze and then the plastic mask was heated up so the plastic could be shaped over my face. It was made to fit tight, as tight as it could go. In fact when the mask was removed it left imprints on my face where the mask was. They told me if I lost or gained weight at any time during my treatments, I would have to have another mask made. No way, was I ever going to go through that again.

The next day was another trip to John Hopkins for my first radiation treatment. I felt like a scared little mouse. Kim took my hand and we started walking down this long hallway. I was so weak and small not so much physically, but mentally. We made it to the little waiting room and in it was the saddest looking group of people I had ever seen. The first thing I heard was a woman talking to another lady about the person she was with, she had lost so much hair that morning and how sick that person was feeling. I look at Kim and again I have to ask her a question I had asked her before. "How am I going to do this?" About that time the doors from the radiation room open up and this young teenage girl walked out, half of her hair gone. She was crying then I started to cry as well. A staff person called my name and asked for my orange card, I was next. The young girl and I passed each other. We looked at each other and stopped walking and just started hugging each other. Again I look at Kim, and for the last time I say, "How I can do this, I can because she can." I gave the girl a kiss and walked away. I knew I had to somehow find that survivor attitude. I couldn't let myself become a victim. I then entered that room for the very first time, what happens to me behind the doors and in front of those doors is unbelievable, I become two different people. I will explain more about that later.

Behind the doors never got any easier, only worse. As it turns out the medical gauze had to be stuffed into the hole in my face each and every time I had a treatment. And then the mask was put on me so very tight and I would be lying straight out on the table and could not move one little bit. I would then get bolted down to the table unable to get up until someone would help me up. I would be left alone, only me and God. For thirty three treatments I prayed to God asking and believing he was removing my cancer. I would try to concentrate on my prayers, trying to drown out the terrible loud noise of the treatment. Every day when I entered that room it would hurt worse and worse to have that stuff packed into the hole in my face. Everyday my face would get redder and redder it looked like I had the worst sun burn in the world. My eyes got dried out and blood shot and my vision started to become involved. Outside of that radiation room I decided I was not going to act like that scared little mouse not one more day.

I was even more aware of how my attitude was everything. I WAS going to survive this. I needed to BELIEVE that with every fiber of my being. I needed to SPEAK that way, and LIVE that way to SURVIVE. Every morning as Kim and I entered Johns Hopkins we started our attitudes. Kim would hold my hand and help me get my brave on, the survivor attitude. We would start by making ourselves known to everyone. We raised our hands to everyone and said "good morning" to all. The security police, the ladies at the main desk, the parking attendants, the people at the coffee shop; they all knew when we arrived. We walked around like there was no place in this world we would rather be. We purchased "cancer sucks" buttons and handed them out to all of our fellow cancer fighters. It was the way we tried to reach out to others, to help them feel better. We started to develop a strong bond with everyone in that little room and other little rooms as well. Somehow looking into the rooms didn't seem so sad any more. We all had cancer or we were with someone we loved that did.

What everyone else didn't know and I would not admit to, I was still very scared. I was a real big chicken. No one knew how bad I was except my radiation team…and Kim. Little Miss Attitude, the lady that walked around like she owned the hospital but all bets were off as soon as those treatment doors closed. I even had to take medication. I tried to go without it once thinking I should be use to the treatments and I should not have to take the medication. WRONG!!! I almost didn't make it that day. Jeffery, good ole Jeffery, one of my radiation team members had to really talk me through it that day. The reality of it, my radiation team talked me through it each and every day. From the time I was bolted to the table my attitude was not the same. My team was on the job. They played music for me and they would talk me through it. Through the speakers I would hear things like "come on Marilyn, your almost done" or "your half way there." And then I would finally hear, "you are finished for today, another one down." I tried so hard, I would lay there and start praying. I would talk to the Lord and tell him I knew that he was removing my cancer. I truly believed this, but then something would happen I would hear those terrible noises; I would feel so closed in. I was so distraught and knew without the help of my teams support the treatment would have had to be stopped. I would think I could not make it, not one more minute and that heaven was such a beautiful place, my wonderful son was there waiting for me so why was I fighting so hard to go through this every day? But then the treatment would be over and I would be walking out of those doors and my game would be on again with my attitude in place. Everyone thought I was so tough and so strong and said I was giving them strength and inspiration, if they only knew.

The treatments were short, if you were to time them with a clock. Often it turned into an all day event before it would be your turn to hand over your orange card and walk through those doors. Sometimes because it was an extra busy day or one of the machines broke down, whatever the reason there were a lot of hours spent with a lot of dear caring people. As my treatments continued and I started to feel the effects I was told that I was going to lose my ability to swallow, to taste, and to eat. "Oh no, not me" I would say. I would keep my attitude and say, "hey, I am not like everyone else, besides I love to eat way too much to let anything like that happen to me." Kim and I made a promise to each other that after each treatment we would go out to lunch. I was out to prove I was going to beat those side effects, and they were not going to happen to me. I did however lose my eye lashes, eye brows and a lot of hair but hey I still loved to eat! Kim and I no matter how bad I looked or how bad I felt went out to eat after each treatment. One of our favorite places to eat was the Cheese Cake factory. Even Kim's mom Shirley joined us on two different occasions and ate out with us. We tried to talk Rex into making the trip with us; I wanted him to see where I received my treatments and have him meet all of my new friends, but Rex refused every time. My angel Kim was behind the wheel almost every day driving from Boonsboro to Baltimore Monday through Friday and I spent Saturday and Sunday at home.

Finally the everyday trips got to be more than I could handle and we stayed at a wonderful place called Hope Lodge. It was such a wonderful place where cancer patients and a "care giver" could stay for free while receiving treatments. Kim and I walked into this wonderful place and made lifelong friends. Carlton another cancer fighter was the first person to greet us he never skipped a beat about my strange looking appearance. He wanted to hear all about "my story" and was just so positive and upbeat; he was so excited and could hardly wait to see me after my reconstruction surgery. We have not seen each other since but we have exchanged cards. Next were John and Linda a married couple from Tennessee. John was so very sick when we first met and continued to be for the longest time. To be truly honest I would sit back and think he was not going to make it. That was until I really got to know his wife. You could just see the way Linda looked at John she was not going to let that happen. The bond that John and I developed at Hope Lodge only became stronger. He was the person that I felt really understood me and was able to get my thoughts back on the right track when they would go off course. We shared a connection most people don't and most wouldn't understand. It was more than just two people with cancer or two people that was not going to let "this" control them. What can I say about John's wife Linda? What a jewel, she loves life, loves to laugh and to have a good time, she is such a rock. Whatever she does, she does with such passion and in such an unselfish manner. I have seen such growth in her as a person.

I also met a lady named Dorothy. Even though there is not much different in our ages, I always call her "Miss Dorothy" because of the amount of respect I had for her from the very first minute I met her. She was a cancer survivor several times over. She had different kinds of cancer in different areas of her body but what you would know first and foremost about Dorothy is she loves the Lord. She knew the Lord had healed her before and would continue to heal her and she was not worried and had no doubts. Kim, Linda, Dorothy and I became very close friends. Several stories come to mind about her.

One story in particular, when I first arrived at Hope Lodge and met these ladies. I had this cover I wore over the hole in my face. The only way to keep it on was with tape, my face was so sore and hurt so bad the skin would peel off every time I removed the cover to clean the area. My Hope Lodge friends told me to leave the cover off if it was uncomfortable that it would not bother them at all. I was too uneasy to do this at the time. Miss Dorothy said she would help me come up with a better way to wear the cover so it would not hurt so badly. Together we came up with an idea to use elastic string which we could tape on to the cover with loops on the other end that wrapped around my ears. WOW, it felt so much better. We decided to go out and celebrate. We went to this Chinese restaurant that was close to Hope Lodge. We walked into the place the first thing we noticed was how hot and humid it was. In fact, it was so warm that all the tape on my nose cover came off and the cover flew across the room. People turned around and looked at me. My wonderful friends said, "See, it is so hot in here it made the lady's nose fall off!" We all laughed and laughed making this a memory we still talk about today.

I remember walking to Lexington Market, one day to pick up some food. People said how unsafe the area was but we were not afraid or even gave it a second thought. Shortly after we got there, a man walked up to us took one look at me (I thought he was drunk) and said "tell me who did this to you and I will go get them". I told him no one had done anything to me except cancer. At that moment if he had been drunk he no longer was. He went on to tell me his own very sad cancer story.

I think everyone that stays at Hope Lodge receives a blessing just by being there. During the time we were staying at Hope Lodge Kim and her husband had planned a family vacation. I believe it was for about ten days. I felt like a part of me was missing but thank God others stepped up to the plate to be my "caregivers "during this time. They included my daughter Brittney, some dear friends like Kathy, Teresa, and a wonderful friend that I always call grandma (her real name is Jeanie). I will have to say it again, after my experiences at Hope Lodge I was changed forever.

I remember one night a man and women had arrived. The man was to have his throat operated on in the morning. He was so afraid that he would be unable to speak again after his surgery. Somehow even with all the other people at Hope Lodge he ended up coming over and sitting with me at my table. I wanted so badly to be able to lift him up, to make him feel like things were going to be ok. How do you make a total stranger feel better at a time like this? I asked the Lord to help me. I had no idea how to give him the support he so desperately needed. This thought popped into my head remembering all the trash cans while driving into Baltimore having the words BELIEVE written on them. This is how I started, my conversation with him, "My friend, you have to believe." The next week there was a knock at my door and it was the same couple, Robert and Peggy. They wanted to thank me for my words and the comfort I had provided them that night. Imagine that, ME going through cancer treatment with no nose, one big hole in my face, little hair, no eye brows or eye lashes, looking like I had the worst sun burn in the world and God was using ME in that way. I had found the right words and it felt great!

CHAPTER ELEVEN
COMING HOME

The weekends at home while radiation treatments and at Hope Lodge during the week were hard, but nothing compared to when the treatments were over and I was back at the house full time. While receiving treatments, I had to keep my edge about me because my fellow cancer friends, friends from Hope Lodge and the treatment team would still see me. I had to be strong and put on that attitude for them. When no one was watching it was much harder. After the treatments ended I was at the weakest, sickest and most tired state plus at that point I had the least uplifting people around me. I had friends that would call and stop by, church friends that would bring food but mostly I was sitting in that old house with the same old issues and Rex. He still had depression issues, was still struggling to get up in the morning, went to bed at eight and he could not find a positive word to say about anything. He could not and cannot help maintain the house or take care of the kids, not even the simple things like tucking them in bed at night. He did not even try to cook any meals or do laundry. I TRIED TO DO ALL OF THE ABOVE. Rex seemed not to have any idea about how serious my illness was. I said to him, "Don't you realize I could have died?" He said, "No, no one told me that." He began to do things he liked to do, like having yard sales every weekend with the young boy that lives down the street. I thought this was a good idea, at least it was a way of making money, but then he said he never sold anything. To make matters worse, Brittney moves out and moves in with a friend. She was trying to take a step forward. If that was true it would have been ok, but it was not a healthy relationship mentally or physically.

I was able to stay in contact with some of the friends I had developed from Hope Lodge and some of my cancer buddies from that little waiting room at Johns Hopkins. I had great friends like John and Linda, Peggy and Robert, Fran and John, Kenny and Ginger. Just talking to them lifted me up, made me feel better, but remember I always had my game face on with them. Most of the time John and Linda did get to see some of my other side but mostly when I would get really down. You see all of these special friends were also a constant reminder that they each had a partner that was supportive and if something happened to them, the other person would feel like they had lost their best friend. The person that was supposed to be my partner felt like he had already lost his best friend and never gave losing me a second thought. During this time I would tell Rex that we needed to be strong, that the Lord would take care of all of our needs that we would be ok as long as we put our faith in him. The most important thing was coming through all of this intact as a married couple and family. He said "what was most important to him was we did not lose the house; he had worked too hard for that." I said "I didn't think it would matter where we lived or what material things we had as long as we were a family." He disagreed and said he did not want to lose that house that is where he wanted to live.

As far as the friends I had before my life went crazy, I learned very quickly not to judge people on how they reacted to my situation. Let's face it; the loss of a loved one often leaves even the most talkative person speechless but the loss of a seventeen year old so quickly and just a few months later the mom faces cancer leaving her with no nose that is quite a lot to take in.

After my first surgery, when my nose was removed, some of even my closest friends, I no longer heard from. No phone calls, no visits, nothing. There were others that would call sometimes but would say they just could not come and see me this way. On the other hand I had the dearest, kindest friends new and old that just came out of the wood work. There were people I had not been close to in years that were there for me and continue to be there for me to this day. DeeDee was one of these awesome people. Others would take care of my kids like Joyce and Duke, Jim and Dana, Penny and Bill, Arnold and Caroline, Miss Dot, Amber, Jeff and Jeffery. Honestly I do not know what I would have done without people like them in my life. Joyce and Duke were like adopted grandparents, if there was a problem in school and I couldn't be there, the school would call them. They went on field trips when I was unable at which time Raymond had to have someone with him at all times. I was also so very blessed after years and years I finally have a church to call my own. I later joined this church but way before that was possible, Pleasant Valley Baptist church had provided a lot of love, support and many, many prayers to my family then until the present.

With all the beautiful people the Lord had blessed me with by putting them in my life I have learned a very valuable lesson. They were showing me more and more about the person I wanted to be and that was a beautiful person, one that goes beyond skin deep beauty but inside beauty. Most of my true blue friends did not care what I looked like and all of the new people I came in contact with now somehow seem to get strength and inspiration from me. Imagine, the plain Jane, never really being much of anything, now can't ever hide. I wear cancer on my face wherever I go with no way to hide it, or cover it up. Since I stand out in a crowd; I might as well hold my head up high and proud because I will turn heads, I will do it in a way to give God the glory. I will work hard to make myself known as a person worth knowing. I go to bed at night and say a prayer and thank the Lord for my life and the wonderful people he has put in it.

The next stage of my life was my numerous surgeries. The surgeries began as soon as I had healed enough from the radiation treatments. This part of my life continues even as I am writing this book. I believe I have had about seventeen reconstruction surgeries to date. Some long major ones, some short same day ones. Some went exactly as planned, others not so much, once on a ventilator, a few times in intensive care but I wouldn't trade it for anything. I look in the mirror and I do like what I see on the outside as well as the inside now. It has been quite a journey, at times a very hard one, but it has made me the person I am today. My surgeries were scheduled early so I would have to be at Johns Hopkins by 5:30 A.M. Kim and I decided we were going to celebrate each and every surgery. We would go to Baltimore the night before have dinner, stay in a hotel and celebrate the next day's surgery. The very first really big surgery had me terrified. At that point, I was having a hard time turning everything over to the Lord and the very talented hands of my wonderful Dr. Patrick Byrne.

Let me say on the evening of our first celebration, Kim's cell phone rang and she handed the phone to me, it was Dr. B. he knew I was having a hard time. After a few words from him I felt so much better and was ready from then on always to embrace each and every surgery. I realized I was very blessed he was so awesome and up until now I thought only God had the power to create a nose, but my Dr Byrne could as well. He was going to be using his God given talents to do so. I knew God was always in control and Dr. B was ever so talented and they both sincerely cared about me. When I first saw myself after the very first surgery it was hard to believe that one day I could have a real looking nose. After that surgery I had what looked like just a big glob on my face. I had a blood vessel taken from my arm and put into my neck and my leg had skin grafts that were taken. Let's see that's an arm, neck, face, a lot of areas for a nose. There was also a lot of care needed when I got home. I know longer had tear ducts due to damage from my radiation so I needed to use eye drops several times a day. There were many more surgeries after that first for forehead flaps, flap revisions, more revisions, and more skin grafts. My neck was cut at least two more times, more veins removed, rib and ear cartilage removed and used several times. I even had under my breast cut and left over cartilage stored under it for future surgeries. Looking back on all the surgeries a lot of them sort of run together. I was kept pretty busy with all the necessary care and all the in between stuff like CT scans, MRI's and blood work.

Some of the surgeries do stick out in my mind. I remember my September 11th surgery, no not THE September 11th, MY September 11th. It was one of the big ones and planned to take about twelve hours long. I was real nervous about this one. I said," who in the world has the sense of humor to schedule a surgery like this on a day such as this terrible day?" Dr. B waited for awhile and then he came to me and said he wanted to tell me a story. He said "if it had not been for THE September 11th he would never have met and married his wonderful wife." They both happened to be at the airport when September 11th happened, the airport closed, and they met. "September 11th, is the best day of my life!" "Now" he said "Let's do this surgery".

As it turned out MY September 11th was not as good. The surgery turned out to be seventeen hours long; I had a few problems and had to go back into surgery that night for two more hours. However, I am what I am today because of MY September 11th. There is another surgery that sticks out in my mind. I had taken care of all the beforehand testing needed for each and every surgery; Kim and I were to meet with Dr. B to discuss what was going to be done. Right before the meeting, I started having these; I guess I will have to describe them as "thoughts". My "thoughts" were this surgery was not going to go as planned but it was going to be ok. I can't describe the "thoughts", I wasn't afraid, but I just knew I had to share this information with Dr Byrne. When Kim and I meet with him he started saying things like the "surgery was going to take six hours, it was not too involved," blah blah blah. I then shared with him that he needed to think of that as plan A and I needed him to come up with a plan B as well. He looked at me with this very strange look. I told him that I did not know why, but I knew that the surgery was not going to go as planned; it was going to have to be done a different way. I asked him not to worry things were going to be ok, just different than what we thought. I suggested he get a good night's sleep, and to pack a lunch. Even though Dr. B and I have a lot of respect for each other I think this man thought I had flipped my lid.

HOWEVER, the strangest thing happened, after many hours in surgery, Dr. Byrne left the operating room to talk to Kim in the waiting room. He explained things were not going as planned and that the blood vessel he had removed and put into my neck and nose wouldn't work. He said he needed to come up with a plan B. The surgery turned out to be a lot more involved and took a lot longer than expected. In the long run, Dr. B said "what may have originally appeared to be a set back or something with a longer recovery time would actually put me further ahead."

"He would have never thought about doing the surgery this way at first but it turned out to be the best way for me." What were those "thoughts" I had? I don't know, perhaps, it was my heavenly father saying, "Marilyn don't be afraid, I am always in control and I know what is best for you, always trust me". Yes, God is always in control and things were going to be done His way in His time. God wanted so much this whole time to keep letting his presence be known. The stronger and deeper my relationship was with him the easier things were going to be for me and a better witness I could be to others. I will give other examples of God's timing later in the book.

CHAPTER TWELVE
GOALS

On the day I was told I had cancer and how rare it was, my family doctor in Middletown, Maryland, Dr. Agarwal, suggested I make goals I wanted to reach in the future. I decided I wanted to fly in an airplane since I had never been on one and I also wanted to swim with dolphins. Dr Agarwal has become such a wonderful person in my life and she has no idea how big of a part she played in my recovery. I appreciate her! She found a place called Discover Cove in Florida and thus a dream was made. Of course my dream included Kim being right beside me. Unfortunately life threw us yet another curve ball and before we got a chance to take this trip Kim became ill. She has juvenile diabetes and was becoming short of breath regularly. She went for some tests and to make a long story short had to have major heart surgery. She was very sick for many months.

I still had to hold onto my dream, something to work towards. I sat down with my family and we decided Brittney, Raymond, Cassy and I were the ones that most wanted to fly and would be the ones to go swimming with the dolphins. Rex decided he was not interested in going with us. He said he had no desire to fly anywhere. Cassy adds to our dream and says "Florida, that has to mean Disney World." This was all we would talk about every time it was time for another surgery our future plans. Every time I was too sick to do what the children wanted me to do, it was ok because one day I was going to be well enough and we were going to be making our dream trip.

During one of my big surgeries, I had a lot of setbacks. I was operated on to fix my nose, that still sounds crazy but I guess that is plastic surgery for you. Remember I told you about this surgery? They had informed me I only had a 10 percent chance it was going to work because so much radiated skin had to be used. That meant my nose might fall off; really it could become unattached and fall off. So what did I do? When things were really at what seemed their worst, I called AAA travel and explained I wanted to work on the plans for our dream trip. I even set the date; it was going to be November 3rd 2008. I told the lady I was making the plans purely on faith, because at the time I was unable to walk, my nose could fall off at any minute, I had no money, and I wasn't sure how many people would be going. I told her that I was sure that the Lord would provide a way for me to take this trip with my children and we had prayed about it ever since I was told I had cancer. I said that is how my faith works, I said I truly believe it, I speak it, I live it, I dream it, so it will be and we had prayed about if for so long I knew the Lord would make it possible.

When Brittney came home that day I told her I was planning our trip for Nov 3rd and she told me that I was totally NUTS! I reminded her to have more faith than that. I was approved for disability and out of the clear blue sky I receive a phone call from the social security office informing me that my adopted children are entitled to social security as well. I was shocked, I said let me get this right you are calling me to tell me you want to give me money? The way I see it, this had to be a God thing. It was not a lot of money but I said "thank you Lord, this is really going to happen".

Around Oct 5th I asked Brittney to go shopping with me because I had gained some weight and needed to get a few things for our trip. Wal-Mart had their Disney clothes on sale, shorts and tops for $5.00. I told Brittney we also needed suitcases and they were also on sale, so for $39.00 we had all the suitcases we needed. We took them home and packed for our trip. The whole time Brittney is telling me how NUTS I am. "How do you think you are going to pull this off, you can barely walk, and you have no money?" I remind her to make sure she takes the time off from work; I was sending a note to school the next day to tell

Raymond and Cassy's teachers they will be missing some school and so she should have faith.

Sunday came; I decided to wear my special suit, the suit that I had purchased to be buried in. If I was going to have faith I was going to have to have total faith and that meant I had to believe I was not going to need that suit for a while. I walked into church still with my cane telling my church family that I am a survivor. I AM, I THINK IT, I SPEAK IT, I BELIEVE IT, AND I WAS GOING TO LIVE LIKE IT.

The next day AAA calls saying the final arrangements needed to be taken care of, like the money. I told her what we knew at that time, we had four of us and that the money was coming. (I still had no idea how I was going to pull this off). Our suitcases were sitting by the front door, the kid's teachers had been informed and one more thing to do. I decide I needed to take the next steps without my cane. I had been working real hard in therapy; they thought I was almost ready, I thought I was ready. I parked my cane by the door and never touched it again. The next day I received a call from a friend of mine, she said someone had contacted her and told her that they had $1,500 and a note that said it was for me and my kids to take my dream trip.

Our trip began the day we had planned November 3rd.and was better than we could have ever dreamed it to be. The only thing missing was Kim. This was the trip that made the fight I had been fighting all worth it. It kept us from feeling sorry for ourselves since we had missed out on so much living. On Sunday November the 2rd the four of us pulled out of the driveway heading to Baltimore, we were going to spend the night close to the airport so we would be sure to arrive on time for our flight. Up, up and away, then landed in Orlando and headed straight to the All Star Music Resort. Everything was just amazing, I sat on the bed and started to cry, our dream was coming true. For a short time my heart sunk, now what? What do you do when your dream comes true? The first place we visited was downtown Disney. Leave it to Disney World to answer my question! I immediately spot a row of jackets with Walt Disney World, Year of a Million Dreams 2008.That was the answer, people are not suppose to have just one big dream . You need a lot of little dreams and a couple big dreams as well. I decided I was going to have to make more dreams big and little. At this point I began looking for the jacket in my size but they didn't have one. Brittney being the shopper she is made sure we didn't miss a store looking for my Year of a Million dreams jacket with no luck. During our stay at the resort I shared my story with the staff in the gift shop asking for help in locating one of those jackets for me. Before leaving that wonderful place I walked into our room and there was a gift basket from the staff with my jacket and a lot of other Disney goodies included. A note was inside saying my story had inspired them and wanted me to have this. So if you spot me walking around I will most likely have my Disney World Year of a Millions Dreams jacket on.

I also dream now of maybe going back one day in better shape for walking. My daughter now wears a necklace that says "BELIEVE". Have Faith my friends, real faith. Believe it, think it, speak it, live it and survive. My very special friend Caroline had shirts made for all of us to wear at Disney that said those very words. Thank you my special friend, lots of love.

I guess now would be the time to explain this is my rewrite of this book. The first time I wrote this book I wrote it in a matter of days and I included only positive statements and thoughts. I included a lot of encouraging words I thought would really help other people to deal with the loss of a love one or a serious illness but the reality of it is there are a lot of ups and downs in life. You have to fight against being swallowed up by any one emotion on any given day. You have to remember there is always something good in every given day. If your life isn't challenging, you're not living a life worth living. Here are some examples of things that came to my mind after I made my first attempt of writing this book.

I was standing in the shower, remember that is where I can either have my deepest, closest talks with the Lord or my darkest thoughts confront me. On this day out of the blue I started thinking about the last pair of shoes Josh had worn. I had to find out where they were. He had them on the day he collapsed, and he had them on at the hospital. I brought them home. Then what? I got out of the shower and by that time I was like a crazy person. I was unable to think of anything but those shoes. I look for those shoes everywhere, for over an hour I am on my hands and knees. I was screaming and crying, I was totally out of control. When Colby came home from school and walked in the door, I hardly even lifted my head to say hello to him, but then something caught my eye. HE had Josh's shoes on. I know where the shoes are but, now what? I want to say, how dare you, they are Josh's shoes I have been looking for them everywhere. Before I said anything Colby looks at me with this sad look on his face and said, "I put them on this morning, I somehow felt closer to Josh" then I realized those shoes were at least a size and a half too big for Colby and he had worn them around all day anyway. Colby was having such a rough time as well. We were not even sure if he would be able to keep his grades up enough to graduate in just a few short weeks. Somehow I pulled myself back together and with words that could have only come from a loving God; I told Colby that it was ok that he was wearing those shoes. However, I wanted him to work hard on filling those shoes. He had to be a good person, work hard, and make himself proud and his family proud. He needed to always show others respect. That was the kind of person Josh was. Colby did go on to graduate from school, he even received three awards. Unfortunately, after graduation Colby made some bad choices and refused to live by the rules of my house and that of society, I had to ask him to leave which was so very difficult.

The shoe day was not the only day that I let myself get really down, there were a lot of them. Another day, I remembered a conversation I was having with Josh and a boy named William. William attended my daycare when he was young and had grown up around my house. Anyway, this conversation happened just weeks before Josh passed away. We were sitting around my back yard and I felt like they were telling me all of my faults as a mom. What they really were saying was, I could be described as an "in your face" kind of mom. They told me they were teenagers and needed to be able to make choices and decisions without so much input from me. They also said if they did make a bad decision or choice about something, it did not mean that I had failed or done anything wrong. They thought if they did something wrong on one day it did not mean that everything was not going to be ok by the next, every mistake was not a major one. They said these words with as much love and kindness as they possible could, but it was just the kind of day I was having. I started feeling like Josh must have thought I was not a good parent and maybe I should not have adopted the other two children. I tell you, the devil was having his way with me that day. It didn't take me long to realize I had to do something about this way of thinking. I was going to force myself to do something about it. I got my list of parents out who had lost a child and sent out cards to let them know I was thinking about them. One family came to mind, their child was killed because of drug activity. I started thinking about what Will and Josh had said. I wanted that family to hear those words, they did nothing wrong, children make choices, what happened was not their fault. Even though their situation was different from mine, a lot was the same and we both lost someone we loved and we had done nothing wrong. I found when I was at my worst the best thing for me to do was to reach out to someone else, to see if I could somehow make someone else feel better.

Something else I have learned there is always someone that has it worse than you do. No, I am not talking about my cancer. Well, yes there are so many different kinds of cancer, some worse than others, some harder to fight, some treatments worse than others but it is more about people's situations. Mine was bad, I mean I had lost a son, just adopted two children and so on and so on but I was still one of the lucky ones. I had Kim, my faith, people in the community; I was not doing without anything I really needed. In so many ways I was still so very blessed. I remember seeing the babies; the little babies that needed cancer treatments were so hard. I would think about the parents of those babies and them needing to let their babies go through those doors. One day I met this young guy, he came in for treatment in hand cuffs and leg irons with two police officers at his side. Kim and I tried to reach out to this young man, to say that we cared and that God cared but we were not allowed to get close to him. We could not even think about giving him one of our cancer sucks buttons. So maybe my situation wasn't that bad. I wondered if that young guy had cancer first or did whatever land him in handcuffs happen first. Maybe it was finding out he had cancer that made the second thing happen. I also think about the young boy that didn't have anybody to drive him to his cancer treatments and he was forced to take the bus back and forth no matter how sick he felt. I remember the social worker trying to help make other arrangements for this person because he was just too sick to continue riding the bus. Yes, I was so blessed. Yes, these were most certainly very challenging years, extremely difficult and such a struggle at times. The family was struggling to figure out how to live without Josh, I was fighting for my life everyday to earn the privilege to be called a survivor. Meanwhile Rex had a back injury that required surgery. I had another situation pop up where a lump was found in my breast and I had to have tests to find out if I had yet another kind of cancer. These were all situations I had elected to leave out the first time I tried to write this book. I decided to add some of it because it shows a little more of what my life was really like. It also tells how much ones attitude affects your well being.

When I was told there was a lump in my breast and needed more tests I said I am just not going to worry about this. I believe that worrying is a waste of time. I said Hey you can't take off my boob; it has some of my nose still under there!" Remember, I had cartilage stored under my breast for a future surgery? By that time I figured I could do whatever I had to do because I already had the most visible form of cancer I could possibly have. I had my nose removed and had to walk around where everyone could see my battle scars so if I had to face having my breast removed, I could do that as well. Everything turned out ok, and I was told that I needed to follow up like every other woman should. Thank you, Jesus. Again, I will have to say we are so blessed. During this whole time neither Rex nor I had been working but somehow we had not gone without. Our needs have always been met. Our mortgage has always been paid, we have not been hungry, and we have not been without heat, or electric, and we've always had running water. Rex sees things so differently his thinking was this sucks, he feels ripped off, his son dies and he feels like he has lost his only friend, back problems, he can't work, and this was his frame of mind every day, all day. Our relationship continues to get worse, we do not argue, we just don't talk to one another. On the rare occasions we did talk, that is when we ran into problems.

Rex still questions everything that has happened to us over the last few years. Why did Josh die? What if this was different and what if that was different, why this and why that. If one or two of our conversations were like this it would have been ok but that wasn't the case. It was all of them and my way of thinking was so different. The Bible has taught me that God does not make mistakes and you have to have faith even when you do not understand. We are just human; we will never understand everything that is what faith is. If you believe that Jesus hung on that cross and died for your sins then you have to believe the rest of the bible as well. You do not get to pick and choose what you are going to believe, I do believe and I believe with my whole heart, not just part of it. It became harder and harder to hear only negative from Rex when I was trying so hard to be positive and to teach our children the right ways. I miss Josh very much, I still cry for our loss also. However, I am so very grateful that the day Josh passed he was happy; he knew he was loved, he was spending time with his family, he was doing something he liked to do and he was saved. I know Josh is in heaven. Josh had been a very special gift from God. He was on loan, just like each and every one of us. It was his time to go home to his heavenly father, his creator. There are times I am almost numb towards Rex.

A friend of Rex's, Pat, stopped by the house, during their visit Pat said to Rex, "your wife is still beautiful, tell your wife she is still beautiful." Rex did not say a word he just looked at me. During my many trips to Johns Hopkins, Rex always said he couldn't drive me there even though he had lived there before many years ago. This used to upset but I tried to understand. On radiation days I invited him to come with us making sure he understood he would not have to drive. I just wanted him to see where I was going, meet my new friends and have lunch. He never went with us, which really hurt my feelings. I no longer care he is not involved with my illness or my wellness I am just so grateful others are. I expect nothing from Rex any longer. I do not expect him to care for the children, cook meals, clean the house, nothing. I felt my best when I was well enough to do it myself and I did it whenever I possibly could. It was very obvious our lives were never to be normal or boring again.

What is normal? I think normal means a wasted life, a life not worth living. Your life should always have a passion in it. Life is good, everyday sometimes you may have to look harder to find the good but it is always there. It is your attitude that decides how long you look before you see it. This says a lot about what kind of person you are. I feel so blessed when people make delicious meals and show up at my house, or when I receive nice cards and letters. People even held fundraisers to help us with the bills we had no other way of paying. When people took care of my children when I couldn't or even when I could they did it just because the love they felt for them. How could I not feel blessed with Kim in my life? Yes Kim, she took me to treatments, doctors appointments and things like that but it was deeper than that. She had cancer right along with me. No, not physically her body did not have it but it became as much a part of her life as it was mine. We were fighting this battle together. How could I not feel blessed when it came time for my kids to start school and I was unable to go out and get school supplies and new clothes for my kids but others took on that task and my kids had new clothes and everything needed and then some. Another friend of mine wanted me to look and feel as healthy as possible so without accepting a penny she would do my hair for me. I was still having surgeries and the circle of events that go along with that like physicals, CT's, blood work, follow up etc. After my surgeries I would be told to keep my head elevated for a certain period of time. There were many times I slept in my recliner because that it where I felt the best.

As Rex and our relationship drifted further and further apart, the time came to never return back to the bed we once shared together. It was a California king size bed which once it seemed as though the bed was huge and now even with that imaginary line drawn down the middle, we were much too close. It was much too difficult to physically be that close when mentally and emotionally we were miles apart. I kept praying that somehow I was going to be able to help Rex. I did get to the point that I stopped doing a lot of things for him I always had. I started to resent it and came to the conclusion that I could not do it any longer if I felt so bad afterwards. I did continue to cook all family dinners and told him that he needed to come to the table to eat with everyone, or I would make sure there would not be any left for him. During this time there were a lot of good things happening as well. Rex, Cassy, Raymond and I had been attending Pleasant Valley Baptist Church. I was asked to give my testimony and it was such an honor. I was so scared that morning. I had not written anything down and as I was waiting to be called up front I was trying to remember what I wanted to say. I could not remember anything. My mind was blank; I was wishing I had written notes. I sat there and asked the Lord to please give me the right words to say. About that time I was called to go forward. Once again, the Lord answered my prayers. Give God the glory. The right words just seemed to flow out of my mouth. People said I was an inspiration and they found it helpful for me to talk with them. Shortly after that Sunday I decided I wanted to join that church. I was in my late forties and had never belonged to a church before; I don't know if I really ever belonged to anything before. It felt awesome.

Rex said we could no longer afford the payments on my car I had been driving and he sold it, I had nothing to drive. That vehicle had been used to get me to all of my medical appointments. On the anniversary date of my nose removal, April 3rd, my church gave me a beautiful 1978 white Toyota Camry. What a blessing that was and on the mirror hung a necklace that said "Believe". How true was that? I never had to look far on any given day to find a blessing. My bottom line, live life, be happy, life is short. You just don't know how short it may be, every day is a gift, don't waste it. Rex's point of view and attitude was still so different from mine. He was doing better in some ways, he was getting out and going places; like going to the movies or out to eat. He was laughing and seemed to be having a good time. He started feeding the dogs. One day I remarked since you are doing better, and was able to do all of the fun things, maybe you should have some responsibility like doing your own laundry. At first he asked "why?" I said I just had way too much to do he finally agreed to do his laundry.

My daughter Cassy and I were watching television one day when a story about a lady with cancer and two young children came on. The story continues and the lady loses her battle and passes away. Cassy looked at me and said "I have to ask you a question." Her question floored me. She said, "Mommy, do you HAVE cancer or DID you have cancer?" After I thought about it for a second, I told her I always wanted to make sure I told her the truth. I shared I was feeling good, the hope was when my nose was removed and I had the radiation treatments that all of the cancer would be gone. Of course I knew the cancer could come back anytime, anywhere. But what was the right answer to this question? I told Cassy I would ask my cancer doctor and tell her what he said. Two days later I went to the doctors and asked my doctor that oh so important question and told him why I needed to know the right way to answer it. The truth is I have cancer. I am only the second person with this kind of cancer. However, Dr. Byrne is a plastic surgeon and always gives great advice "Live life" it was that simple with him. I do not think he ever gives a thought that cancer is still so real for me. When I got home I told Cassy the doctor said the answer is I still have cancer. I asked her not to be scared that I was ok. I am doing everything I can to stay as well as I can and my doctors will help me with that. What she really needed to know was I loved her very much and I will love her even more tomorrow and even more than that the next day. I said no matter what, she would always be taken care of. She looked up at me with those big beautiful eyes and gave me a big hug. I knew she appreciated my honest answer. I had shown her she could always count on me and she could always trust me. That was huge for her to understand.

I have been living in a revolving door. I have either been getting ready for a surgery, healing from a surgery, planning a surgery or thinking about my next surgery. There were always follow up visits, stitches or staples out and more trips to Johns Hopkins. Days are very busy just taking care of all my medical needs. When I was not in the hospital, the care I needed was unbelievable. When I had the big hole in my face the scabs had to be picked out of that area several times a day. The areas of surgery needed to be kept very moist, putting medications on it several times a day. There was wound care that needed to be done to my face and skin graft areas. I am so thankful to people that would help me when I needed help. Penny, who was also a nurse, would come by keeping an eye on my progress. If there were changes she would often notice them before I would, like signs of infection. At times, my daughter Brittney would have to help me take a shower and with skin graft care. I never dreamed my daughter would have to be giving me a shower, at least not until I was quite elderly. Nicole was also on standby and if I needed her I knew she would come by.

One of my biggest fears during this time was being able to breathe. Of course, I could always open my mouth but for my entire life, that is what I used my nose for. When I had the big hole in my face there was no problem and I could breathe through that. The problem began when the surgeries started. When I shared my concerns with Dr. Byrne, I just wondered, as much as he always seemed to be in control of everything and every situation there must have been times that had been very difficult for him. First, my case has been very rare and I was always putting my two cents worth in. He understood how important this breathing thing was for me and he kept coming up with ways to make sure that every time I woke up from surgery, I was able to breathe through my nose. It did not matter what kind of nose I had.

This continued to be a very difficult time for Raymond and Cassy. When they would see me after a surgery it was very hard for them. Cassy wouldn't say much and sometimes that would make me worry even more about her. Raymond would walk into the room and stand way back away from me. He would say that I "looked very scary" and that he could "smell it". After a while he would say that he knew it was still me because I sounded the same. He then would come closer and give me a kiss and walk away. A little later he would come back and sit with me and then not want to leave me for a long while. I found out that the children would worry about me if they had too much information but would also worry if they felt like I was hiding something. I would always wait until the night before I was scheduled for a surgery to tell them about it. I did have to make sure I told them about every trip I made to Johns Hopkins. I think this really helped them feel I was always honest, in control and that everything was going to be ok. Another thing that was hard was when there were special activities at school. Raymond would say I shouldn't go because I would scare the other kids. As time went on, I realized Raymond was trying hard to protect me and my feelings. I did go to many meetings at the school regarding issues Raymond was having until he entered First grade because things were somewhat better for him then. It wasn't until December 2008 that Raymond requested that Brittney and I go to the school to see him in a holiday program. He said some of the kids might still be a little scared but he thought it would be ok. One thing that was so helpful to me during this time was a very special gift I had received.

My friend Penny started from day one to take pictures of me and my journey to make a scrap book for me. Whenever I would start to feel a little down I would look at my book and be reminded that I once was dying from cancer, I once had a nose, and that every day needed to be thought of as a gift. Just look at me now. Earlier I said I wanted to share more about God's Time. In January 2008, after many reconstruction surgeries, I finally had what looked like a nose but the worst possible thing happened. It fell off, it became unattached, right where the bridge of my nose should have been, it came undone. My doctor explained there was nothing that could be done to stop it or prevent it or fix it at that time. The doctor said there was too much damage from the cancer and treatments. How does that saying go? It is what it is. I really tried to keep as upbeat as possible for someone whose nose was falling off. No, really, I was blessed; after all I was still alive. My doctor were trying to make a new nose using my own body parts, ribs, cartilage, skin, bones, vessels, and arteries. Setbacks should be expected, right? I should still feel blessed even though I had to admit it did get tough. I lay in bed one day feeling really sad and down. My wonderful doctor had told me it was going to take months for me to heal before we could move on. Here I am with another hole in my face, exposed cartilage, what a mess. It had been months like this. Me and my ever changing appearance, this was not a good look for me.

Penny came over to help with the necessary medical care and she took pictures like always. The pictures were real graphic; parts of the skull base showing, exposed cartilage, and the gaping hole where the bridge of my nose was suppose to be. We talked about how the doctor said it was going to take months to heal and how much difficulty I was having with the thought of that. After Penny left I went back to bed and I started praying. I told the Lord about my hard time, but how I so trusted him, and that I was turning everything back over to him. This was too big of a problem for me to even think about any longer. I knew it was not going to do me any good to worry over this matter. I told the Lord I was so ever grateful for where he had brought me and that I had faith to know he is always with me and that he is in control. I thanked him for the talents he had given to my doctors. With this said I went to sleep. The next morning I got up and prepared to start the everyday terrible care that was required to take care of the exposed cartilage, the hole, etc. This morning was different when I looked in the mirror, I did not see the exposed cartilage nor did I see that big hole. My eyes were damaged from the radiation, so whatever the reason I did not see......not to worry. That is the promise I had made to the Lord the night before. I had turned everything over to him. I walked out of the bathroom and did not give it a second thought. The next day came and I got up prepared to start my day and medical care. Again, I couldn't see anything exposed no hole. So what was going on? Could the cartilage have fallen out without leaving a hole? I had turned everything over to the Lord but I started to back track just a little. I started to feel a little scared so I called Penny. She laughed at me when I asked her if something could have fallen out. She told me she would be over after work that evening. I asked her to make sure she brought the pictures she had just taken, not even 24 hours ago and her camera. When Penny arrived another one of our friends was also there. Her name is Dana. First, I showed them both the pictures Penny had taken just twenty four hours before. I then took off my bandages and both ladies had a hard time believing what they were seeing at first. I was healed! There wasn't anything exposed and the hole had disappeared!

CHAPTER THIRTEEN
GOD ANSWERS PRAYERS IN HIS OWN TIME!

As I am writing this I still have a little way to go. In fact tomorrow I will have another cancer test and following week scheduled for yet another surgery. One of the first things I do every morning is to thank the Lord, the next thing I do is shave my nose. My nose and the area around it grow hair faster than any man can. This happens because of the forehead flap but my insurance will not cover the cost to have hair removal. So I will embrace everyday with open arms and a razor in my hand and be glad I have a nose to shave. Attitude, I have always tried to keep a positive one. Sometimes you just have to laugh. As I am sitting here right now I am thinking about my tubes. They have been a part of my life since my very first reconstruction surgery. The tubes are these plastic hoses which are inserted into my nose holes to keep them open so I can breathe through my nose. At first they stayed in all of the time, only taken out to be cleaned. Guess who had to take them in and out and clean them? Yep, it was me. In the beginning, especially, it really hurt because the tubes are pretty big and long. To look at them, it was hard to believe they had to be pushed up into my nose, no matter what kind of nose I had at any given time. I had to always remember the thirty second rule. My thirty second rule was, it was going to hurt like the dickens for thirty seconds while I shoved those tubes into my nose, but boy did I love the way I could breathe after they were in.

As time went on and my nose improved, my tubes got a little smaller and now I am at the point where I can take my tubes out and not wear them in public. I still put them in when I sleep just to keep everything nice and opened up in my nose holes. Yes, I am sitting here laughing, I just have to. These tubes have put me in strange situations where all I could do was laugh. One time after I woke up from a surgery, different tubes were put into my nose and they looked like I had two lifesavers sticking out of my nose. When people would look at me, they would have to look twice.

When I cleaned my tubes I would soak them in an old plastic sour cream container that I would have sitting in the bathroom. One day, my God daughter Danielle came over and asked me why I didn't keep my sour cream in the refrigerator like everyone else, why did I always keep mine in the bathroom? Another time the tubes put me into a funny situation was at the pharmacy. I used lubricating jelly like KY jelly to insert the tubes into my nose. Rex and I were at the pharmacy; he was on one side of the store I was on the other, Rex was to grab the lubricating jelly while picking up something else from that area. Well he yelled across the store "what kind of this stuff do you want?" I responded back to him, "I don't care I just want to be able to stick those things up my nose!" It was not until everyone in the store started looking at me in such a funny manner that I realized what a blooper had just occurred. What did I want to stick up my nose? Ha-ha, all I could do was laugh.

I remember a time when I had just gotten out of the hospital and looked terrible, I had stitches all over my face and neck and I had the really big tubes hanging out of my nose. Thank God it was also Halloween. I was able to go trick-or-treating with my children, grandchildren, family and some very dear friends. I must say, I had the best costume and I sure turned heads, others were very jealous. To think I almost didn't go that night, until I had an attitude adjustment. I was thinking I looked too bad, and felt too sick to go out. I was not going to miss that night with my loved ones when I had been given a second chance at life. Sometimes an attitude adjustment is just what we need and I have needed a few.

I was making cookies with Raymond and Cassy one day. I had really missed doing that with the kids. I use to bake a lot with the children, not only my own but my daycare children as well. I was so glad this day that I was well enough and to make cookies together. This turned out to be a disaster in the kitchen. They looked terrible; I burned almost everyone of them. I was getting so upset, what was wrong with me. I then decided that this was nothing more than a waste. I decided that since those cookies were a disaster we would make No Bake Cookies. Well, that wasn't working out so well either. The No Bake Cookies were not getting hard. About that time I receive a phone from an attitude adjustment his name was John. I have talked about my friend John a few times. He said, "I bet your kids really do not care what the cookies look like or even that the cookies are not getting hard, what really matters is the three of you are together. I bet that is what is really making them happy" Well let me tell you, when I got off the phone, Raymond, Cassy and I ate those No Bake Cookies with a spoon they never did get hard, but they were the best cookies we ever had. Adjustments always need to be made.

I told you about how sick Kim had gotten, and how much of a rock she had always been for me. When she got sick I was like a fish out of water for awhile. She had been my emergency contact person, she knew every one of my wishes and dreams, she knew my doctors, and their phone numbers she even knew what I wanted to have happen if I should die. I was surprised how dependent I had become on her. I knew she had my back and that I could always count on her. Miss Joyce and Mr. Duke were always there to care for Raymond and Cassy but they were going to be out of state for a while. I couldn't do this alone, what was I going to do? I was about to be educated again. I had to learn to ask when I needed help and realize it was ok not always to appear to be so tough. Things started falling into place. Other wonderful people came forward to take care of my children like Caroline, Mr. Arnold, Miss Dot, Amber, Dana and Jim. Brittney would come to me and ask the date of my surgeries and the dates of my follow up appointments. Brittney and I even went to Baltimore the night before and celebrated surgery. It was wonderful to share this experience with Brittney. I learned some very important things. Brittney was able to see a different side of me. Let's face it, when someone is getting ready to be wheeled into an operating room they really have a different appearance as they lay there in their little hospital gown and paper hat. Brittney got to see her mom being human. There are times when everyone feels a little weak, or not in total control, where they have to act on faith. People can be tough as nails or as weak as a toothpick.

I started to realize maybe I had spent way too much time trying to be so tough around my family because I thought it was the best thing for them. I thought it would make them feel safer and since I appeared to always have everything under control, everything was going to be ok. Looking back, I know there were times when I should have asked for their help, but I thought asking for their help was a sign of weakness. I thought if they didn't offer help it meant they did not want to help. Let me go on record as saying I was wrong.

I will give one big example of where my pride and being such a hard head almost caused a lot of damage. It happened right after my leg was operated on, taking blood vessels, veins and a big huge skin graph off to use in making my new nose. I was unable to walk or bear any weight on the leg at all. I was learning how to walk with a walker with the help of an in home health care worker. Brittney went out that night, leaving Rex and I home alone. I had a room downstairs fixed up with a hospital bed so that I could keep my leg elevated. Rex said he was going to bed and walked upstairs to his room. At this time I was still sitting in the living room. After he went to bed I decided to go to my room, I stood up with my good leg on the floor, and this was still very new and very hard for me to do. I picked up the cordless phone thinking if something should happen, I would be able to call for help. I tried using my walker and one leg to walk to my room. I made it about two steps and took a very bad fall, I was so mad at myself! I knew I had risked my whole recovery and all the progress I had made because I would not swallow my pride and ask for Rex's help. He did hear me fall and came down stairs and helped up me, I came close to hitting my face on the hardwood floor. My leg was so bandaged up I really could not tell at that time if I had done any damage or not, but it appeared to be fine. Rex did help me to bed for the next few nights until I was able to get around with my walker better. He would bring me a bottle of water and the phone each night. So, I got a little better asking for help when it came to the fear of falling.

Finally about a week after surgery I began physical therapy and regained the use of my leg. I was still unable to ask for help with the laundry. I had been in the same clothes for two days. Finally, when Brittney came home from work one day I asked her to get me some clean clothes because I was unable to get to them with my walker. She wanted to know why I had not asked her for help before and I really didn't have an answer to that question. I guess I really had to learn to ask for help. I had always been the one helping and doing for others before I got sick. I was still trying to reach out to others when I was well enough to do so. I really had to work hard to learn to give others a chance to give a blessing as well. It had always felt so good to help others I had to give others the chance to help me. It is about learning to give as well as receive a blessing, it has to work both ways. Sometimes people really wanted to help and they just didn't know what to do so if I needed help, I needed to learn to ask those that wanted to help. I needed to learn to accept the help that was given.

CHAPTER FOURTEEN

We were all learning so much about giving and receiving but mostly about Christian love. This in itself was so amazing for my children to witness first hand. I was having a hard time deciding where to add this into my story. Again it was something I had left out the first time I wrote this book but after a lot of thought I think it is something that is really important to be included for many reasons. I am hoping that people understand how important my relationship with the Lord is. How important it is for me to be a Christian. Does this mean that I am perfect, not by any means? Are there any perfect people in this world? Again, the answer is no, we all fail every day. We can start a relationship with God at any point of our lives or reestablish a personal relationship at any time. We all fall short of the glory of God, we are only human. When we are born again, our sins have already been forgiven, past and present. Now, as I have throughout this book, I will give an example.

I had a very dear male friend of mine that I had known for over twenty five years. We have not seen each other for over twenty years but we would e-mail each other back and forth on occasion. This was someone who always talked of having a great respect for me and would always make me feel much appreciated. The long and short of this is, in 2006 there were some inappropriate e-mails exchanged between this person and myself. It was only words and nothing more. These e-mails ended up in Rex's hands and after awhile he confronted me about them. I was not, however the first person he had told. I explained to him they were words, nothing more. I explained how he should have known this. How I had never left the house at any time that could not ever have been unaccounted for and never without the children. He agreed this was true. I explained how this was a way of filling a void in my life at that time. I cut off all communications with this person. I never change my e-mail information so it could be checked at anytime. Rex hid the printed copies of the e-mails. He told his family members and other people that I had an affair and that I was going to leave him. He said he would take these e-mails to the preacher of the church and to other church members to show them what kind of person I really was. He wanted to prove that I was not a Christian and that I am nothing more than a phony.

Now, why is this so important for me to share? First, Rex made me feel so badly and for the longest time I was afraid he was going to "expose me." Again, all I really needed was an attitude adjustment. Yes, the words exchanged between this person and myself were wrong, but I was already forgiven by the one that really mattered. That was my Lord and savior. I asked for forgiveness and I received it. I was giving Rex way too much power over the situation. The people he was telling "Marilyn was having an affair" stories to, were going to believe whatever they wanted to believe. If Rex decided he wanted to show the preacher or my church family the copies of the e-mails, so be it. They loved me. We all fall short; they would not feel like they would have to judge me just as they would not expect me to judge their short comings. We do not have to answer to each other.

So folks, don't let anyone play those kinds of head games with you. God loves you with all of your short comings, hang ups, and imperfections. He has a desire for a personal relationship with you. It is his forgiveness you should ask for and desire and you will always receive it. Be prepared, forgiveness is kind of a funny thing. It is one of the hardest things we may ever be asked to do. Rex and I have been married for twenty three years, during those years he had done a lot worse things than write e-mails to someone. I had forgiven him or had I really? I thought I had, but the minute this issue came up; I was ready to open those old wounds. That is not really total forgiveness. When we ask the Lord to forgive us of our sins, we are truly forgiven. Even though I thought I had forgiven Rex of his past indiscretions, I was ready to bring them up in a heartbeat. As Christians we are to forgive others just as Christ has forgiven us. I had always thought of it as a gift we give to that person, it helps them feel better. That is only part of it. It may help the other person feel better but one thing for sure, if you can really forgive someone you will truly lift a burden from your own heart. You will never find true happiness until you forgive others for the wrongs they have done to you, or against you.

I have talked a lot about being a survivor or surviving, what does that mean? Does it mean you live, and you will not die? Of course not, not really. Everyone will pass away one day or another. When I say survive it does mean to live, sort of. It means to make the most of each and every situation. You should always find the good in everything. Be a good witness, and stay strong in your faith. A true Christian can almost always be picked out of a crowd. They are not sad and gloomy. Even in their hardest times they handle it in the best of ways. I once had someone tell me they didn't know what I had but they wanted some of it. What did I have? If you are reading this, you have read my story, and what did I have? I have changed, very much so. I have become stronger and happier more now than ever. I have always appreciated the little, simple things in life but now they make me scream "Thank you Jesus!" Just to stand in the shower and have water run over my face. Wow! How awesome is that. You must be thinking I am nuts. But after my first big surgery and after a lot of the little ones I was not allowed to get my face wet. Just imagine not being able to get your face wet. I now sometimes just stand in the shower for what seems like hours, letting the water run down from the top of my head, over my face and feel like I am one of the luckiest people in the world. When I finally get out of the shower and I look in the mirror, I see that I have eye brows again. Man, isn't that great? I have been given a second chance at life, I will not waste it.

We have even found a use for those pink little basins the hospital gives out after each surgery. Brittney, Cassy, Raymond and I each have one with our names written on them. We take the time to have family nights which ours is a little different than most. We sit in front of the television, soaking our feet in our pink basins with nice warm smelly stuff in them. After we are finish eating we take turns giving each other a foot massage. Life is so good. When the kids ask for macaroni and cheese for breakfast I do not feel the need to explain that pancakes and eggs are breakfast foods. In fact, I have learned that on rare occasions it is ok to have dessert first and the main meal second. I have found great joy in giving myself a birthday party and really celebrating being one year older. The kids and I sit on the hill behind McDonalds and feed the birds French fries and have so much fun. I sure give thanks that I have been at the hospital for the birth of each of my grandchildren. I can only imagine where life may take me to next.

The year 2009 started out very sad. My dear, close friend Caroline passed away. Caroline and her family would often take care of Raymond and Cassy when I was in the hospital and Miss Joyce and Mr. Duke couldn't. They would have the kids over to their house quite often because they really loved the children......and me. I became very close with the entire family and shared a lot of things with Caroline which hardly anyone else knew about me, she was one of my strongest supporters. When Raymond, Cassy, Brittney and I were getting ready to make our dream trip to Florida, it was Caroline that had shirts made saying, BELIEVE IT, SPEAK IT, LIVE IT, and SURVIVE. That was a possible title for this book. When Caroline got sick I wanted so badly to finish the book so I could give her a copy for Christmas in 2008. She was sick in the hospital with all indications she would be home for Christmas, that didn't happen she never made it home physically. Now, she is in her heavenly home. I had such a hard time with this but more so poor Raymond and Cassy had another big loss. Again, it was a person that really was not an old person, or a person that had been sick a long time. You know when you explain death to children you usually use examples like; people get old, or when people get real sick and people are in pain for a long time.......That was not true for Josh and was not true for Caroline, the only person it seemed to be true for was me and I was still here. Things were also getting so much worse between Rex and me.

You see, I finally decided a person is only going to live up to what you expect of them. I thought back to Josh, it was very clear what was expected of him and every one of the children, and they always worked very hard to do what was expected of them. Colby was ok when he was doing what was expected but when that changed he had to pay the consequences for the choices he made. Raymond was expected to do what all the other kindergartners' were doing even when he was living and had been living in a crazy mixed up world. For Cassy, the same thing was true. You have read my story. As for Rex, we expected nothing. He always told us because of his depression he was unable to do anything. Well, that had been ok for all of this time, but I started feeling like it was time to expect more. He had been going out to eat, going to the movies, going to carnivals, and to church. I felt he should not just be able to pick and chose what he wanted to do. I felt it was time to expect him to take part in regular family duties. It was not fair to the rest of us that he was able to choose the fun stuff when everyone else had responsibilities. I believed he was not doing enough to improve his mental health condition since he felt he was unable to do even simple little things around the house. My thoughts were he needed to be a person that Raymond, Cassy and Brittney could feel like they could depend on. I also wanted the kids to know that I believe that in life they can do anything they want to if they want to do it bad enough. They should never let anything get in their way. I never let the children say "I can't" but that is all they heard from their dad. This only made life between Rex and me even more difficult.

The other part of my life continues on as it had been. After my next surgery in March when it was time to come home, the situation between Rex and I was so bad I found myself sending Raymond and Cassy to their room's to protect them from all the "grown up" stuff. I couldn't stand it at that house anymore. I finally felt like I was reaching my breaking point. I truly felt like I was living with my worst enemy. In my mind I was thinking that I had to get out of that house, to take Raymond and Cassy and get to a healthy environment. How would I ever be able to do that? I didn't have any money. I figured I would just be stuck here. I said "Lord, what am I going to do?" "I can't take this anymore!" A friend of mine Arlene called, she was telling me how she had this trailer on her property and the lady who had been renting from her had moved out. She now has this two bedroom trailer that has just become available. God has just opened a door. I open up and tell her about my situation and ask if I could become her new tenant. On April 3, does that date sound familiar? It is the anniversary date of my original surgery when my nose was removed. It was also the date my church gave me my cute little Camry, and now when I am so desperately in need of a fresh start; it was also given to me on April 3rd.

Leaving my house after twenty two years was still hard but I can honestly say as God as my witness, I had always been a faithful wife during our marriage. At no time had I ever been touched by another man and had not been touched by him for many years either. Of course it did still cause a lot of hard feelings when I left. My new little home is perfect. It is only ten minutes from the old house. The kids did not have to change schools, or lose their old friends, they just made new ones. I didn't take anything but clothes with me when Raymond, Cassy and I left that day.

When I explained to Raymond and Cassy that we were leaving that house and were going to live in another one, I said we were going on an adventure. I let them know we were going to a place we could be happy, with no screaming, and we would be looking out for each other and have each other's back. I told them one day we might decide to go back to the old house but for now the trailer would be our new home. We were there for weeks with no television, no video games, nothing like that. We read a lot of books and played homemade games like bowling with water bottles and socks rolled up for balls.

Raymond and Cassy each have their own rooms. I have a dresser and closet space in Cassy's room. I sleep on the couch in the living room, and I sleep like a baby. Raymond tells everyone how happy he is and how he wants us to stay at the trailer and live forever. Cassy chooses her words a little more carefully but goes outside and plays and in many ways seems as though the weight of the world has been lifted from her shoulders. Rex does not understand how I could possibly be so happy in a trailer. He is still at the old house we shared for all of those years, surrounded by all the stuff we collected for all of those same years. That is what has always been important to him. I live in a two bedroom trailer with two beautiful children that I did not give birth to but God gave to me as a special gift.

I have a good relationship with the rest of my children and grandchildren. (Jimmy, I wish was better). I have very little belongings, YET, I am so very happy to be working on my future. I do go back to the old house to take the children for a visit. It does not mean the minute I moved out I had given up on my marriage. I thought it might cause a good reaction with Rex. I hoped Rex might realize I believed he was throwing away everything that really mattered, and he might feel the same way. Just maybe he would wake up in that old house and see that I was gone, Raymond's room was just as it had been but no Raymond and Cassy's little princess room looked the same but the little princess didn't sleep there anymore. When that didn't seem to move any mountains, I thought maybe the first holiday, which happened to be Easter, would.

I had always made such a big deal out of each and every holiday. I would always fix big meals; have company over, made a big fuss. So when Rex came to me and asked what I was doing about Easter this year, since we were living apart, I told him he could have Easter this year. It could be at HIS house and he could handle everything. I told him he was in charge. Things turned out very nice. There was a ham dinner and Brittney hid Easter eggs filled with candy. After we finished eating, Rex got up from the table and cleared the dishes and loaded them in the dish washer. When the day was over, I told him how very nice things were and that I was very impressed. The next day he called me and again I told him that the kids had so much fun and how nice everything was. I remember saying, "You should be very proud of yourself, you really proved to yourself that you could do a lot more that you ever thought you could". He said, "See I knew you were going to say something mean, I just knew you couldn't say anything good" and "You should know, Brittney did most of the work." We have not had dinner at either of the houses since.

What does my future hold for me? I have not figured all that out yet but this isn't what I want to talk about yet. What I want everyone to know is everyone is a survivor, a survivor of something, if they choose to be. It could be of a dysfunctional family, of abuse, divorce, the loss of a child, or cancer. I am a survivor of all of these things. Everyone has their own demons or maybe even many demons. It's like someone being born without an arm; they are only going to be a victim if they choose to be. You can be your biggest supporter or your worst enemy. I was, and still am very determined not to be a victim, not to anybody or anything. I could have allowed myself to crawl under a rock when my son passed away, or I could have thrown in the towel when I was told I had cancer just a month later. Heck, I could sit back and do nothing now, but then what kind of life would that be? I truly believe everyone can survive whatever their situation is, whatever they are faced with. The secret is they truly have to want to be a survivor. You have to really, REALLY want to, you have to BELIEVE you can, you have to SPEAK out loud your desires and you have to LIVE your life in a way that shows how serious you are about your plans. It can happen for you the same as it happened for me.

Another example is a battered person, if they really decide they want things to be different, I mean really decide they are ready for change and for their lives to be different, and then they do the same thing I did. First, they have to BELIEVE, their life can and will be better. They have to be able to close their eyes and see their new life away from the abuser, and have the vision of what their future looks like. Next, they need to SPEAK out loud what their future will be, what their desires are. They have to BELIEVE and SPEAK the way it will be. They need to decide and then say this is what I will do and have done to me; this is what I will not have done to me, not by anyone. Say, "I BELIEVE IT with every fiber of my being, I am a GOOD person and I am WORTH it. Stand in front of a mirror and say it, stand in front of others and say it, over and over again. "I am a good person, I will not be mistreated, I will not be hit, I will not be talked mean to, etc" The next step, and it is important, LIVE your life in a way that says what you speak. Hold your head up, shoulders back. Don't forget dress the part, make sure your hair is done in a way that says, "I am a survivor, I am in control, I am a strong person, I will not be a victim, for anyone or anything. I would also suggest that everyone have someone to call. Everyone needs a support person or group. You should have someone to call to help in tough times, be a survivor. You can do it just like me. You see, you and I are so much alike, our DNA is the same. We both come from a loving GOD that has given us everything we need. What I have been through has most certainly been a journey, but I have been victorious. You can be as well.

At a very low point in my life right after my dear friend Caroline died I felt like I was ready to really just fall apart. She was a person who knew me so well; I had shared so much of my life with her. She knew of my day to day troubles. I was at a point in my life where I felt like I was almost living a double life at times. Most of my church family had no idea how troubled my home life was. Everyone on the outside thought we were one big happy family. Caroline said there was a song called "Tough" that reminded her of me. But boy would she have been disappointed in me. On the lowest of low days I found myself sitting in the doctor's office saying, "you have to give me something I am falling apart." I told my doctor I had been in bed for two days and my friend Caroline had passed away and I needed something to take or I would not be able to go to her memorial services. I started crying like flood gates had opened up about some things that had been happening at home. This doctor said something very important, he said, "Who are you protecting?" "Why do you feel like you have to keep all of this a secret?" "You are not looking out for the right person." I learned a very important life lesson; Abuse stops when secrets stop. My dear friend had not even been buried yet but she was still finding a way to make sure I made positive changes in my life. Thank you my friend. Life is truly so much easier to live when you are living the truth.

Start today; turn your troubles over to the Lord. Your slate can be wiped clean and you can start your life over in a new meaningful way. Raymond, Cassy and I call our little trailer our home and where Rex lives, the old house. I went to the old house a few months ago to try and have a conversation with Rex. He said he missed having us there. I asked what he missed; he said when we watched TV together which was about an hour together in the evening. I asked him what a marriage meant to him, he said "two people sharing the same bed." I asked " What do you feel when you look at me?" He replied, "Nothing." I told him I would not be moving back to that house and if I ever had any doubts, I did not any longer. I knew the marriage was over. He could have said anything to me except, the word nothing. I left and went back to my new home and my new life. The old house never felt like my home ever again. It wasn't the same place I had lived for twenty three years, it felt like the place that Rex chose to fight to keep instead of his wife, his marriage, his family and maybe even a meaningful future.

Is this a case of men looking at things differently than women? Maybe it was. Rex says he worked years for that house and he was going to keep it no matter what. He thought our main problem was I did not have a true understanding of depression. At this point the only thing I was struggling with was; I had been very good at turning every situation of my life over to the Lord, every area except my marriage. I guess I had gotten to the point that I truly felt the marriage was beyond repair. I often looked at a copy of a letter I had sent Rex not long after I moved out. Once again I was trying to make him understand that my moving out had nothing to do with anyone else other than the two of us. He still felt like he had to blame someone other than taking any responsibility himself. He still refuses to accept any responsibility for our failed marriage; he says it has all been his depression. I was still trying to get him to understand that although things were very different now, we still had a lot to be thankful for. He just does not get it!!

A lot of people say that many marriages fall apart after the loss of a child. So many people ask and or assume this is what destroyed our marriage. I guess I want to share some of my thoughts on marriage and divorce. I am going to say something that may sound strange at first but I really do not believe in divorce. However, I do not believe in marriage at all costs either. People say they stayed together for the kids. I now believe, sometimes that is the best reason for two people not to live together. There are times when a mother and father living together can cause more harm to a child. There should also never, EVER be abuse, either physical or mental in a relationship. I also have to say that the worst excuse someone can give for walking out on a marriage is "I was not happy." If you are not happy, you do not have the right to blame your unhappiness on someone else. You are responsible for your own happiness. No, the death of Josh did not destroy a perfect marriage; in some ways not even a strong marriage or even a good marriage.

What I mean is I could not make Rex responsible for my happiness that was my job. I could pray for us to have the kind of togetherness and closeness that I wanted but if Rex was unable due to his depression or whatever the reason, it was still my responsibility to be happy within my marriage. As you probably have figured out by now, I was a note writer. I wrote Rex a note one time, sort of a thank you note. I thanked him for allowing me to get all the Christmas stuff out of the basement-all by myself and putting up the tree-all by myself. I also thanked him for allowing me to prepare, cook and clean up after ever holiday meal as well as to do all the dishes-all by myself. I explained how fixing every meal, everyday was such a treat. I also thanked him for never holding my hand as we walked on the beach.

I did have choices to make. I could decide not to have big holiday meals, not to do all the decorating that make the house look so beautiful or I could decide to not go to the beach every year, which was such a blessing. I had to change my attitude and know I was blessed to have very many friends that loved coming to my home and having meals with me, a beautiful home to decorate and vacationing at the beach every year, which I loved. Rex did go to the grocery store with me, except in the last few years, and did pay for the vacations. Were there things I would have changed, absolutely?

So back to did our marriage fall apart because of the death of our son? NO. It did become very unhealthy and more out of control. It crossed into abuse as defined by medical professionals. It became unhealthy for me as well as for our two young children. It was not me just being unhappy. I truly believe the Lord will forgive me for leaving my husband.

On the wall in our new home there is a hanging that reads "If you can dream it, you can do it". Also in our living room there are the letters that spell out the word BELIEVE. We have a statue that Kim had given me and on the bottom is hand written I have your back. My children and I are starting to dream again. Raymond has a hard time with life. He has some very serious mental health issues. He has required the services of mental health professionals and medications. Along with this I watch his diet and exercise. What he is allowed to say out loud is also very important; we try to use positive statements about him and others. I truly believe with the right resources and with his desires, there will be no stopping my smart little guy. Cassy and I will one day make a Christian mission trip to Africa. There are a lot of obstacles standing in our way in making that dream happen but there were just as many when we started planning our trip to Florida. So, look out Mr. Mike and Miss Arleen, when you go to Africa on one of your upcoming trips plan for Cassy and I to be there to help with the water wells, to help in the orphanage and to spread the word of God to anyone that we can get to listen.

I do not expect our lives to be easy. I walked away from a house and its "stuff" when I was to be fifty on my next birthday. I have yet another surgery next month. I have made choices that some may not be able to understand but I made them to live the kind of life I feel was best for my minor children and myself. I truly believe the Lord still has wonderful things in store for me and I will continue to live my life in a way that will glorify him. The children and I will be just fine; we will not just land on our feet we will be ready to get our feet moving. Do I still feel like I gave up too soon on my marriage and saving Rex? No, as bad as I feel, I do really know in my heart I have tried everything I could and I will continue to pray for him. I still try to talk to him about choices he has made and about being the kind of person that would make himself and his children proud. I try to SHOW him not just talk to him about being a Christian and showing Christian love.

At Thanksgiving time, I received a call from Boonsboro Elementary School saying a local church had given my children and me some Thanksgiving food. I later received a call from Linda and Wayne, lovely friends from my church, asking if they could bring over some things for us. They also gave us Thanksgiving goodies. After praying about it, I decided I should give Rex a Thanksgiving basket of food. I had plenty of room for it and the children and I sure could have used it after the holiday but I felt like we had been given an extra blessing and it was up to us to pass it on. I called Rex and told him we had a Thanksgiving basket of goodies for him. He told me he wished he had "a thermometer to tell him when the turkey would be done", so I went and got him one of those as well. I must say, I think he really did appreciate what I was trying to do and it sure felt good doing it.

Thanksgiving turned out wonderful. The children and I were invited many places for Thanksgiving but we decided to just spend a quiet day at our little home. This was quite different for us. At the old house, I would have had many people over, a lot of noise and a big meal. We had decided to go with just the big meal. After eating, Cassy and I took the dog for a walk; Raymond decided he did not want to come with us. On our way back home we started picking up sticks. At that point we had no idea why. When we got back to our little trailer we came up with the idea of using those sticks to make crosses. They turned out to be beautiful wooden crosses that the three of us decorated for Christmas. We were able to take basically nothing and turn it into something very beautiful. We gave many of those crosses away as gifts. Later we were told that people had wanted to buy them from us. We could have sold them but decided to give them to anyone that asked for one, as a way to honor Josh and his memory.

I guess the bottom line is I realized everyone makes choices; God gave us that wonderful right. However everyone will be accountable for the choices and decisions they make. I have to understand I guess there are some people that will not be open to my testimony. You see when Jesus comes into your heart you are a changed person, you have a desire to live your life in a different way. Trying to deal with some of the emotions that I have had to deal with has not always been easy. Sometimes it can be the little things that really get under my skin and can make me a little bitter if I let it. I am still working on being a better person every day. Christmastime was a little hard but caused me a lot of growth. I invited the kids and grandkids over for our Christmas meal and to exchange Christmas presents. Rex was also invited and came as well. Brittney also invited a dear friend of the family. I tried very hard for everyone to have a good time and made sure everyone received gifts. When Rex was ready to leave I asked him if he could take the trash with him to his house. I do not have trash pick-up at my home. He said that "he couldn't take it because he was going to the store and did not want to have trash in his truck." He asked that "I have Brittney's friend take the trash in his truck." So I took the trash out and put it in ….Rex's truck. I know I still have some growing to do. I told Rex, "I found a place in the back of your truck for the trash, and it doesn't look to bad, thanks". He thanked me for inviting him and left.

Your life will not always be a bed of roses, you will still have trials and tribulations but you will know that you always have the love of God with you. Your hard times will always be easier when you know you are not fighting them alone. As the year 2009 is ending and 2010 is beginning I am so looking forward to what the New Year has in store for me and my children. It is by no means starting out perfect but whose life is. As for Rex, he claimed personal bankruptcy. He said he also bankrupted Blank's Cleaning and Restorations but "don't worry, work can still be done by R & B." He is still living at the old house with Brittney. He has filed for disability and he has a roommate paying rent to help with the mortgage.

Tonight, when I tuck Cassy in bed, she will start her prayers off by saying "Thank you Lord for this wonderful day," like she always does. Raymond will tell me how much he "loves me." These are the things that really matter and are most important in life.

I know there has been enough healing because the children and I can now sit around and tell little memories about Josh without crying or feeling sad. Raymond remembers how Josh used to hook his power wheel to his four-wheeler so he could take Raymond for rides all through the woods. How Josh would tease Cassy because she couldn't say "Happy Easter." I know I have the love of Jesus in my heart and when people look at me they can say, "That lady must be a Christian" even if they don't know me. I know all things are possible with Christ the Lord and I won't believe all my good days are my yesterdays. I hope that I have somehow touched you in ways which have enriched your lives. Any battle that you are fighting can be made easier if you just look up. Look up to the sky and open up your heart. My dream is that by reading my book you will know that all things are possible with Christ and you will have a desire to seek out a personal relationship with the Lord Jesus Christ. You too will then have eternal life and someday we will meet in a beautiful home called Heaven. May God bless you sincerely. I have been having earaches and a growth in my neck causing a lot of pain which as of April 2010 it has been confirmed my cancer has returned. My surgery date is set for April 12, 2010. I AM STILL LOOKING UP!

Manufactured By: RR Donnelley
                     Momence, IL USA
                     November, 2010